To All God's Beloved
in New Haven

David Bartlett's Yale Sermons, 1990-2003

To All God's Beloved in New Haven

David Bartlett's Yale Sermons, 1990-2003

Edited by Ian Doescher

To order additional copies of this book, contact:
Xlibris Corporation
1-888-795-4274
www.Xlibris.com
Orders@Xlibris.com
21688

Contents

Introduction 7

January 23, 1990 · Yale Divinity School ·
Psalm 104:24-34, Acts 1-2 9

September 5, 1990 · Yale Divinity School ·
Matthew 24:45-51, 2 Corinthians 4:1-7 15

October 28, 1990 · Battell Chapel · Matthew 22:34-46 23

October 11, 1991 · Yale Divinity School · Mark 2:1-12 30

November 21, 1991 · Yale Divinity School ·
Matthew 28:16-20 35

April 17, 1992 · Battell Chapel · Luke 23, Isaiah 53 40

May 25, 1992 · Yale Divinity School ·
Deuteronomy 8:1-20, John 6:52-71 46

March 4, 1993 · Duke Divinity School ·
Jeremiah 9:23-24, Matthew 20:1-16 51

September 2, 1993 · Yale Divinity School ·
Isaiah 55, Romans 1:8-17 55

August 14, 1994 · Battell Chapel ·
Ephesians 5:6-20 60

November 27, 1994 · Battell Chapel · Luke 21:25-36 67

June 25, 1995 · Battell Chapel ·
1 Kings 19:1-18, Luke 8 74

September 22, 1995 · Yale Divinity School ·
Luke 15:1-10 82

October 8, 1995 · Battell Chapel ·
Habakkuk 1:1-4, 2:1-4, Luke 17:1-10 86

May 27, 1996 · Yale Divinity School ·
Acts 2:1-14, 1, Corinthians 12:1-13 93

September 6, 1996 · Yale Divinity School ·
    Luke 10:38-42, 1 Corinthians 14:13-19 100
December 8, 1996 · Battell Chapel ·
    Isaiah 40:1-11, Mark 1:1-8 106
October 30, 1997 · Berkeley Divinity School ·
    Matthew 5, Revelation 7 113
April 10, 1998 · Battell Chapel · John 19 119
September 18, 1998 · Yale Divinity School ·
    Exodus 32:7-14, Luke 15:1-10 126
September 23, 1998 · Berkeley Divinity School ·
    Psalm 119:33-40, Proverbs 3:1-6,
    Matthew 9:9-13, 2 Timothy 3:14-17 131
May 24, 1999 · Yale Divinity School ·
    Jeremiah 31, Mark 16:1-8, 2 Corinthians 4:1-6 137
October 20, 1999 · Berkeley Divinity School ·
    Isaiah 45:1-7, Matthew 22:15-22,
    1 Thessalonians 1:1-10 142
December 8, 2000 · Yale Divinity School ·
    Luke 3:1-6, Philippians 1:3-11 148
August 28, 2001 · Yale Divinity School ·
    Mark 1:1-8, Hebrews 11:32-12:1 152
October 7, 2001 · Yale Divinity School ·
    Habakkuk 1:1-4, 2:1-4, Luke 17:5-10 157
November 1, 2001 · Yale Divinity School ·
    Matthew 5:1-13 164
May 27, 2002 · Yale Divinity School ·
    Genesis 1:1-13, 2 Corinthians 4:1-12 169
September 11, 2002 · Yale Divinity School ·
    Matthew 5:1-13 174
January 31, 2003 · Yale Divinity School ·
    Isaiah 50, Mark 6:47-52, Galatians 3 178
May 25, 2003 · Yale Divinity School ·
    Jeremiah 31:31-34, Matthew 28:16-20,
    2 Corinthians 3:1-6 182

Introduction

It is an honor and a privilege to call myself the editor of this collection of sermons by David Bartlett. I am not the first to have thought of putting a collection of Dean Bartlett's sermons into a book, but I am fortunate enough to have asked him about it at the right moment.

This collection includes 31 of Dean Bartlett's sermons preached at Yale during his time as Professor and Academic Dean at the Divinity School. Like Baskin Robbins 31 varieties of ice cream, you are likely to find your favorite David Bartlett sermon in this collection, sermons you've recognized and enjoyed, and sermons that are completely new to you. And, as in the selection of an ice cream flavor, it is my firm belief that you should try every one—and often.

When I first considered this project, Jennifer Creswell (my wife) challenged me: "Why do we need another collection of sermons by a heterosexual white man?" Jennifer's point was well taken, and gave me pause. The reason I pursued this project is twofold: first, this book is primarily intended for members of the Yale community who have known Dean Bartlett during his years here. Dean Bartlett is dear to the Yale community, just as Yale as a collection of students and as a University is dear to him. This fact is so evident in his sermons, as he often refers to the congregation as "beloved" or "dear friends."

Second, Dean Bartlett is an excellent example of the kind of man heterosexual white men should be. Behind his professional and jovial exterior, Dean Bartlett is a deeply sensitive and compassionate man. He is careful to be respectful and inclusive in his sermons—for instance, he always uses gender-neutral language for humanity and for God, and always refers to his wife Carol Bartlett, as "Carol Bartlett," as opposed to "my wife" or "Carol," as so many other preachers might.

If I had one suggestion to the reader, it would be to read this book with the Bible close at hand. Anyone who has taken a preaching class with Dean Bartlett or heard him preach knows that the text is central to his sermons. Therefore, these sermons are best—or perhaps most truly, according to Dean Bartlett's method of preaching—experienced if you can read the biblical passages before you read each sermon.

Beyond that, enjoy these 31 varieties of Bartlett. So many of us have been touched by Dean Bartlett and his sermons, and this collection is equal parts appreciation of his homiletical skill and appreciation of the person he is.

Ian Doescher
Yale Divinity School

January 23, 1990 ·
Yale Divinity School ·
Psalm 104:24-34, Acts 1-2

The first sermon of the collection was Dean Bartlett's candidacy sermon, as he applied for a position at Yale. This sermon was preached in Yale Divinity School's Marquand Chapel, where members of the Divinity School community gather on a daily basis to worship, on January 23, 1990. Virginia's Union Theological Seminary, mentioned in the opening sentences, is the institution at which Dean Bartlett taught prior to coming to Yale.

I

Watts Chapel at Union Theological Seminary in Virginia betrays its southern Calvinistic heritage. To call the sanctuary austere understates the case. A dark wood chancel rises above dark wood pews. There is a central, dark wood pulpit. No cross adorns the chancel. No icons complicate the windows, and the only decorations on the wall are granite tablets memorializing deceased presidents of the Seminary.

Worship in Watts Chapel is often rich and edifying, but usually also in a solid, sober way. One suspects that John Calvin would be pleased.

Just before we began our observation of the Week of Christian Unity at Union, a student led a service that tested our unity more than the traditional interdenominational prayers of more recent days.

He confessed that he was a Presbyterian charismatic, and he sought to lead us in worship that reflected the tradition that meant so much to him.

Because I know and respect that student and know and respect friends from many different communions whose spiritual lives have been deepened by the charismatic movement, I wanted to service to work. But, the sad truth at that time and that place is it seemed to cut too much against the grain. Folk accustomed to the Geneva Psalter had a hard time with happier choruses designed for guitars. Folk nervous about kneeling or even standing to pray became visibly anxious at the thought of raising their hands toward heaven. And when the most supportive among us did clap hands at the appointed time, the sad truth is we had the noise but not the beat.

In that place, at least, among those Presbyterians, the joy of the Pentecostal movement did not translate very well; what should have brought us together made us feel, I fear, rather far apart.

I puzzled whether the Pentecost story depended for its joy on charismatic fervor, or whether there might be in that charter narrative the signs of an even deeper joy, which could unite not only Catholic, Protestant and Orthodox, but charismatics and traditionalists alike.

II

Here's what I think I found. The joy of Pentecost, the unity of the Spirit that comes to the church at Pentecost, is the joy of conversation. Of being able to talk with one another.

"When you send forth your Spirit," the Psalmist says: "All things are created." What the Spirit creates at Pentecost is community, conversation.

"And at this sound, the multitude came together, and they were bewildered, because each heard the apostles speaking in his or her own language. And they were amazed and wondered, saying: 'Are not all of these who are speaking Galileans? And how is it that we hear, each of us, in our own native language?'"

We are learning, partly from teachers in this school, that as Christians we are a community of language, bound together by words, images, affirmations.

Yet surely what we want to affirm is that what binds us together is Christian language; language that acknowledges denominational differences but reaches beyond them: if the Spirit can let the Gospel be spoken and heard among Parthians and Medes and Elamites, Mesopotamians, Phrygians and Pamphylians, then surely the Spirit can keep the conversation open among Catholics and Lutherans and Presbyterians and Brethren and Baptists.

A recent journal presents excerpts of a debate between Carl Braaten of Lutheran Theological School in Chicago and George Lindbeck of this school: the debate is on the best setting for the training of new Lutheran pastors. Braaten argues for the exclusive validity of denominational seminaries, Lindbeck for the virtues of denominational communities in University Divinity Schools.

My own guess, having worked in both settings, is that each is appropriate for certain students. But, what has disturbed me in Braaten's article was his attempt to quote George Lindbeck on his side; Braaten claims that because faith communities are communities of language, we learn best in those communities which speak our language. "As Lindbeck says," quoth Braaten, "'one learns to speak French best in France.'"

But I should think that the deeper problem of our time is not to learn how to speak Lutheran or Anglican or Baptist but to learn to speak Christian; that our confessions are, if you will, the dialects of a common conversation.

The virtue of this kind of school is that it waits for the Spirit, or perhaps even nudges the Spirit to keep the conversation going—to make of the Church, not just of this denomination or that, a communion, a fellowship. Those of us who work in different kinds of settings depend on this place and a few others not to be satisfied with denominational enclaves, however rich their heritage.

If one danger is that we shall be separated from one another by denominational language, there is the deeper danger that we shall be separated from our people by clerical language: "And they were amazed and wondered, saying: 'Are not all these who are speaking Galileans, and how is it that we hear, each of us, in our own native language?'"

Here John Calvin helps: "If the preachers of the Gospel had spoken one language only, everyone would have thought that Christ was confined to a small corner of Judea."

Truth is, most seminaries and Divinity Schools teach one language, if not exclusively then overwhelmingly: it is a good and necessary language, the technical language of our trade, and you need to know it. Eschatology (future or realized), substitutionary atonement, *heilsgeschichte*, *redaktionsgeschichte*: you are learning it all.

But going from this place whether as teacher or preacher, chaplain or social worker, you will wait on the power of the Spirit to lead you and gift you to speak the language of the people where you will witness. To find the words and the images and the stories which will NOT rob the Gospel of its power but which will acknowledge its beauty, and anchor it in the real lives of your people.

The Spirit will not only help you speak to those people; the Spirit will help you HEAR them, to hear the words that mask and reveal the way they see the world. The language of the lips which hints the language of the heart.

Six months into a new parish, the church treasurer stopped the pastor outside the church. "When you first came here," said the treasurer, "I said to myself, 'She knows her stuff.' Now," he said, "you're beginning to know us."

It is not enough to know the language of Galilee, of this small corner of the church where you are studying. You will need to learn the local languages of the places where you serve, so that you can interpret texts and share faith.

Unless the Spirit grants you to speak languages people can hear, the sad truth is this: they will not really understand what you say. And the second truth is like unto the first: neither will you.

III

The joy of Pentecost is also this: the joy of being able to bear witness to the mystery of God in Jesus Christ.

Jesus gives that astonishing promise to the apostles: "But you shall receive power, when the Holy Spirit comes upon you, and you shall be my witnesses in Jerusalem, and in Judea, and Samaria, and to the end of the earth."

Our unity is this: that the Spirit calls us and empowers us to be witnesses. To bear witness to what we have witnessed—heard, seen, touched, felt—the love of God come in Jesus Christ as near as flesh and blood as bread and wine.

Our unity is this: the Spirit calls us to be witnesses to those who are far off, but also to those who are near at hand. To the community of the Church.

The Spirit calls us even to bear witness to those who have witnessed to us: to pastors, teachers, friends, families, to those given you to love and serve in this place and to those given you to love and serve in other places, other times.

"You shall be my witnesses," saying in Jesus Christ the judgment and love of God have come near as flesh and blood, as bread and wine.

Four years ago, as it often does for parish ministers, our vacation fell apart. So we ended up camping near Santa Cruz, California, and on the last day of vacation headed for the beach.

Some of you may know the scene. From the parking lot you come first to the boardwalk with its aging roller coaster and dubious Ferris wheel, a fake Popeye and costumed Olive Oyl working a crowd. The greasy food followed by stomach-threatening rides.

And then the beach, not one of California's cleanest. Cans and papers sometimes simply left where they were used, sometimes dropped near the garbage can but not quite in.

But then, beyond the boardwalk and beyond the beach—the Sea, great and wide, which teems with things innumerable, living things both small and great. Beauty beyond our ability to make cheap. Wave after wave breaking in power and delight upon the faint rim of the shore.

We sat watching our sons dig at the water's edge, and turning saw this sight:

A woman, perhaps fifty, with her daughter, perhaps twenty-five, walking slowly down the beach. Between them, the mother's mother, daughter's grandmother, well along in years, arthritic, lame. They led her, brought her, bore her slowly, gently down the beach.

Decades ago, we can guess, this older woman brought her daughter to the shore and helped her learn to love the sea. And then again, more recently, grandmother and mother came back to the ocean, bringing the little girl.

Now they are grown, mother and daughter, and the mother's mother, no longer able to lead them—she is led by them down to the glory of the sea. And the mother held her mother, and the daughter knelt and took off her grandmother's shoes.

And then together, arm in arm, they led her across the edge into the cool, shallow wash of infinite sea.

So do we all, by the power of the Spirit, dear friends, one by one, each in our turn, lead one another to the fringes of the glory of our God.

To God be thanks and praise.

September 5, 1990 ·
Yale Divinity School ·
Matthew 24:45-51,
2 Corinthians 4:1-7

*In his first month at Yale Divinity School, Dean Bartlett—
then Professor Bartlett—preached the following sermon,
titled "Ministry by Mercy," as part of the Divinity School's
convocation ceremonies. In this sermon we hear about
Florence Darby, about whom we hear more in the sermon
preached on October 30, 1997.*

I

During the years that I was a student here I was much
sustained by worship in this Chapel and by the wisdom I imbibed
from my mentors in classes and at the coffee hour that followed
Chapel. But I was also nourished by the minister and people of
Calvary Baptist Church where I did field work. It was a small
church struggling to survive, worshipping in what is now the Yale
Rep, held together by the power of prayer and the interest from a
modest endowment.

Let one picture stand for a host, one name for a modest
multitude.

Each Friday afternoon I went to call on shut-ins or on church
members with particular pastoral needs. Most Fridays I ended

my calling on Osborne Street where Florence Darby lived. Early in my time at Calvary Baptist, Floss had lost her beloved only sister to cancer. During the months of illness and bereavement we grew close and stayed so. I stopped each week to speak a word of cheer and to receive one, too.

According to an apparently random timetable, Floss sent me from Osborne Street back to Prospect Street with a freshly baked apple pie and a round package with six wedges of cheese. The cheese was not distinguished, but the pie was—a gift to me and to the community dwelling on the first floor of Bushnell House.

Uncannily, the pie always arrived just when we most needed it: when some crisis of academic preparation or of vocation or even of faith had hit. Just then, at what we knew as students of Greek or Tillich was the *kairos*, just at the proper time our self-absorption was interrupted by tart apples, flaky crust and cheese wrapped in foil. A gift, a grace, a mercy.

II

"Who then is the faithful and wise servant whom the master has put in charge of the household to give the other servants their food at the proper time?" At the *kairos*.

Matthew uses Jesus' little parable as a picture of church leadership, of ministry, in his own day. And as a picture of ministry it is not bad at all. We are called, invited, to give just the needed food at just the proper time. Food for thought and food for faith. Bread broken with thanksgiving. Wine shared in remembrance and hope. Music against scared silence. Comfort just at the moment of mourning. Joy just when celebration reaches its peak.

"Who then is the faithful and wise servant whom the master has put in charge of the household to give the other servants their food at the proper time?"

What makes us ministers—parish ministers or teaching ministers, ministers of music or ministers of social service, actual ministers or potential ministers? How does it happen that we are invited to provide the word of grace, to share the bread of mercy at the proper time?

We speak of call, and that is part of it. We speak of gifts, and they are part of it. But Paul, defending his apostleship, gives us another word, too. "Therefore, since it is by God's mercy that we are engaged in this ministry, we do not lose heart." You can translate it more quirkily: "Therefore, since we are *mercied* into ministry, we do not lose heart."

Mercied into ministry, just as we are mercied into faith and into baptism and into the church. Mercied into salvation and mercied into justification and mercied into vocation, too.

We have known for a long time that you can't slip a hair's breadth between Paul's conversion and his call. It was all one as surely as we are graced into faith, and what we are in danger of taking so pompously and piously and seriously was for him, even on the worst of days, joy, gift, mercy.

Karl Barth, who was often not as serious as his students, wrote of the mercy of being a Christian and therefore of the mercy of being a Christian minister as well: "The Christian is the one who will always be the most surprised, the most affected, the most apprehensive, and the most joyful in the face of events. He will not be like an ant that has foreseen everything in advance, but like a child on Christmas Eve."

We are mercied into ministry: mercied into sharing God's food with God's people at the proper time.

As he wrangled with supposedly apostolic opponents, Paul knows exactly what food the people most need: "We have renounced the shameful things that one hides. We refuse to practice cunning or to falsify God's word, but by the open statement of the truth we commend ourselves to the conscience of everyone in the sight of God."

In my favorite Frederick Buechner novel my favorite character is a woman named Rooney, a parishioner who confronts her minister named Nicollet. "There's only one reason come stumbling in there week after week," she says. "I want to know if it's true, just true, that's all. And that's the one question you avoid like death."

"We provide ministry by the open statement of the truth," says Paul.

Here in these halls and in your ministry present and to come, our loyalty to the truth means that faith seeks understanding. We need not look far to see the dangers when faith closes the windows and builds the barricades. In the Catholic Church we see the struggle over a whole range of issues focused perhaps most clearly in the call to the ordination of women. In the largest evangelical denomination in the country we see the attempt to define faith by an impossible doctrine of biblical inspiration. In the mainline becoming old line from which I come we hear a new version of the old cliché: "It doesn't matter what you believe, just so you don't share your belief with me."

Yale Divinity School is an institution which gifts the church by insisting that the appeal to faith is an essential word but not the only word, a community that loves God with the mind as well as with the heart.

But the truth that feeds God's people is not abstract truth or distant truth for Paul: "For it is the god who said, 'let the light shine out of darkness,' who has shone in our hearts to give the light of the knowledge of the glory of God in the face of Jesus Christ."

In our ministry while faith seeks understanding, understanding seeks faith, too. When we have understood the unique social setting of this biblical book or that, we push on to ask how God speaks from that setting to our own. When we wonder how firm a foundation or anti-foundation our philosophy gives our faith we wait, still, for God's courage to speak, to write, to act—at the proper time.

One of Reinhold Niebuhr's students and friends said of that Christian, whose searchings and doubts and affirmations are public knowledge: "Even when he had the hardest time, Niebuhr always intended to believe."

Mercied into ministry, given the ministry of mercy, graced to proclaim the truth, we always intend to believe. Understanding seeks faith.

III

I love Paul. I love the gift of being mercied into ministry: to declare the truth of mercy, mercy as truth. Perhaps influenced by my many Lutheran teachers here I did and do tend to center my understanding of faith and practice in the letters of the Apostle to the Gentiles.

However, the text we read from Matthew is at last as much about judgment as it is about mercy. We give food at the proper time, but woe to us if we fail. Off we go to join the other hypocrites with much weeping and gnashing of teeth.

In my years here and in all the years since a more Matthean word has always been spoken both publicly and privately by Bill Muehl. As many of you know, Professor Muehl long taught communication and preaching here. Bill thought YDS students in general and me in particular to be so steeped in the world of mercy that we would accept nearly any outrage in the name of God, including, of course, our own most outrageous sloppiness, silliness or laziness.

Never one to let me off the hook, Bill checked up on me from time to time. Once catching a note of enthusiasm in my description of preaching in a new parish he sent a sternly cautionary note. "Before you get up in the pulpit every Sunday you should read Edward Arlington Robinson's poem, 'Richard Cory.'"

I pulled an anthology from my shelf and read.

> Whenever Richard Cory went downtown,
> We people on the pavement looked at him;
> He was a gentleman from sole to crown
> Clean favored and imperially slim.

And he was always quietly arrayed,
And he was always human when he talked;
But still he fluttered pulses when he said
'Good morning,' and he glittered when he walked.

So on we worked and waited for the light,
And went without the meat and cursed the bread;
And Richard Cory one calm summer night
Went home and put a bullet through his head.

I put down the poem and finished the letter. "Now," wrote Muehl, "whenever you get into the pulpit, just remember that what you say may stand between some poor person and utter despair."

Perhaps the word was too strong, but not much too strong. "Who is the faithful and wise servant whom the master has put in charge of the household to give the other servants their food at the proper time? . . . But if the wicked servant says, 'My master is delayed,' and beats the other servants and drinks with drunkards, the master will cut him in pieces and put him with the hypocrites where there will be weeping and gnashing of teeth."

We have been mercied into ministry, by mercy given the gift of sharing the word, the bread, the wine, the counsel, the hope. But we are mercied into responsibility, too. When the people hunger, we are there to feed.

Clearly Matthew knew that—encouraging church leaders who would lead without lording. Goodness knows Paul knew that he was mercied into responsibility. His anxiety for the Corinthians runs almost as deep as his faith in God. He was mercied into ministry, though the churches pay him little heed and more charismatic opponents carry the day.

We are mercied into ministry, though the words we speak seem sparse, though sometimes our folk complain that there is no real meat and curse the poor bread we provide. We are mercied into ministry, sometimes being there at just the right moment but sometimes thinking that some other engagement is more pressing—or marching in with our wisdom or bread or wine or apple pie just when folk least need or want to see us.

We are mercied into ministry. We are mercied into responsibility that we will sometimes botch, whether Christ return soon or tarry, so that there is no hope for us—unless we read the next verse beyond our passage from Paul: "But we have this treasure in clay jars, so that it may be made clear that this transcendent power belongs to God and does not come from us."

We are mercied into ministry, but we are also mercied throughout our ministry, from the first day to the last. As God knows us before we are born and after we die, so the beginning and the end of our ministry and all the days between are, of course, responsibility and danger and sometimes triumph and frequent disaster and always: mercy.

IV

So close with a better poet than Robinson and a better comfort than Richard Cory. George Herbert was an Anglican cleric. He knew as preacher and priest how much he lacked and as Christian how much he owned. He called his poem "Aaron."

> Holiness on the head,
> Light and perfections on the breast,
> Harmonious bells below, raising the dead,
> To lead them unto life and rest:
> Thus are true Aarons dressed.

> Profaneness in my head,
> Defects and darkness in my breast,
> A noise of passions ringing me for dead
> Unto a place where is no rest:
> Poor priest thus am I dressed.

Only another head
I have, another heart and breast,
Another music, making live, not dead,
        Without whom I could have no rest:
                In him I am well dressed.

Christ is my only head
My alone-only heart and breast,
My only music, striking me ev'n dead
        That to the old man I may rest
                And be in him new dressed.

So, holy in my head
Perfect and light in my dear breast.
My doctrine tuned by Christ (who is not dead
        But lives in me while I do rest.)
                Come people; Aaron's dressed.

To Christ be thanks and praise. Amen.

October 28, 1990 ·
Battell Chapel ·
Matthew 22:34-46

The Church of Christ in Yale (United Church of Christ)
meets in Battell Chapel, on Yale's Old Campus. It is the
University Church for Yale University. For many years,
Dean Bartlett was frequently a guest in the Battell pulpit.
This sermon is one of his first sermons for that congregation.

I

"When the Pharisees heard that Jesus had silenced the Sadducees, they gathered together, and one of them, a lawyer, asked him a question to test him." Or, as The Revised English Bible puts it, more pointedly: "One of them tried to catch him out with a question."

The tenured faculty in the department gathered together for the doctoral oral exam. The victim—I mean the student—guesses how little chance he has to pass. He doesn't quite fit the departmental bias. He is an old-fashioned new critic among the deconstructionists, or a foundationalist surrounded by pragmatists. Not only does he disagree with his elders, he is mouthy about the disagreements.

Now he faces the inescapable moment. They are out to get him. One of the professors asks the first question. "Tell me, Jesus, what is the greatest commandment. Name one."

"I'll name two," says Jesus, proving just as mouthy as his reputation. "You shall love the Lord your God with all your heart, soul and mind," says Jesus, "and also, at the same time, you shall love your neighbor as yourself."

The trouble is—from the perspective of the tenured faculty—the trouble is that the answer is absolutely right. They haven't caught him out at all. He may have answered more cutely than they would have preferred, but what he says sums up the great tradition that they share with him. You shall love the Lord your God, and you shall love your neighbor, and if you don't do both you don't do either one quite right.

II

You cannot love God without loving your neighbor, Jesus says, and the tradition he represents and fulfills knows that it is true.

You can't love God without loving your neighbor in a community of faith. You can't love God in splendid isolation. Robert Bellah and his colleagues have written *Habits of the Heart*, a book about the great American escape from community. Religious faith, like so many aspects of our lives, has become more individual and individualistic.

At the climax of Bellah's study we find a woman named Sheila who worships at home by herself. Her religion is called "Sheilaism." "It's just me and God," says Sheila, "what I need and what I care about without needing to check it with other people or share it with other people, either."

One of the great advantages and disadvantages of a University Church, where so many of us are so mobile, is that we can worship next to each other without having to worship WITH each other. The word of the Gospel nudges us beyond our comfortable isolation to find ways to know each other and to share our faith, even in the midst of busy lives, in the midst of a busy University.

You can't love God without loving the neighbor in faith, and you can't love God without loving the neighbor in need. That may be even harder that Jesus imagined. The neighborhood has got so much bigger. That we are interdependent is a truism, in part because it's true. The newspaper can overwhelm you before breakfast, and the TV news can depress you after supper with the word of our global neighborhood.

In my student years here the gurus of the drug culture told us to turn on and drop out. In these later years there has grown up a kind of drop-out religiosity: just me and God together.

The classic mystics always brought the world and the neighborhood to God in prayer, but this new piety uses prayer to escape the world and to avoid the neighbor.

"Now I belong to Jesus, Jesus belongs to me," shades over easily into "us against the world, just the two of us against the world."

But the God who is God comes to us in the neighbor, and will not be found where the neighbor is not prayed for, loved, and served.

Erik Jacobsen is an essayist for *Esquire* magazine. He happened to be in Katmandu when Mother Theresa came for a visit. The posters announced, "Blessings will be given." Because Jacobsen was curious and not averse to blessing, he went to meet her.

As it turned out, there wasn't much of a crowd, and somewhat to his astonishment, Jacobsen soon found himself in a rather short line, waiting to meet the saint. He reached out his hand and mumbled something appropriate and unclear. Mother Theresa took his hand and spoke as clearly as can be: "Can you help?" she asked. He moved on, puzzled, questioned, somewhere at the edge of blessing.

We turn from the needs of our neighbors and the complexity of our neighborhoods to seek blessing and escape. We find in God's presence the blessing which is also a question: "Can you help?"

III

"You cannot love the God who is God without loving your neighbor," says Jesus, this clever student questioned by his academic and theological superiors.

"And you cannot love your neighbor without also loving God."

Now that's the harder one. With good conscience I can stand up here and say that love of God without love of neighbor is empty, thin. But neighbor love apart from love of God—we see that all the time. The quest for justice and the love of mercy, quite separate from any overt religious belief.

And if we say, "oh yes, but those good people are really covert believers, anonymous Christians or closet theists," then we violate the love of neighbor by trying to make these others, these neighbors, over into our own pious image.

So take this not as analysis but as witness, testimony. If the danger of loving God without attending to the neighbor is dropping out, the danger of loving the neighbor without attending to God is burning out.

"Weary with well-doing" is not just a fine old phrase. It's how we can end up at the close of a long week or in the middle of a long life, unless our souls find restoration, strength, encouragement.

Dorothy Day didn't learn about compassion or justice through any explicit faith. Her heart embraced charity and her mind embraced socialism in response to the needs of her inner-city neighbors. But the vision that might sustain others was not quite enough to sustain her. When her daughter was born, Dorothy was amazed to discover her own deep conviction that her daughter should be baptized in the Catholic Church, and her own baffled conviction that she, Dorothy, should be baptized as well.

Her faith grew roots deep enough to sustain the breadth of her compassion. Her biographer writes of how she kept her radical vision and her radical companions but found faith to move her on the way: "Both Dorothy and her friends were seeking community—the final and complete harmonization of all. The difference was that her friends talked of this as something that would crown the revolutionary struggle, that would be found in time. Dorothy came to see that the way was love, and the end was eternity."

For Dorothy Day, at least, the love of neighbor was sustained by love of God. And for my friend Gene Mayers, too.

Gene was deeply concerned to discover and build some stronger structures of justice for our society. So he came first to law school here and then to work on a Ph.D. in philosophy at Columbia.

While at Columbia, Gene began to court Odette, and together they went most Sundays to James Chapel at Union Seminary to hear the faculty preach.

Then came World War II, and Gene went to Europe. As a soldier he was confronted with issues never dreamt of in his philosophy, or his law school, either one. How does one serve justice in the midst of disaster and war? Gene wrote to the preacher he'd liked best at James Chapel, Reinhold Niebuhr, and Niebuhr wrote back.

I do not know exactly what Niebuhr wrote, but his words brought Gene to faith in the God who knows and forgives the imperfections of our justice and our mercy and who sustains us to go on trying.

Gene Mayers is to this day passionate for justice and passionate for God.

IV

The Pharisees came together in a body, and one of them tried to catch Jesus out with a question: "What is the greatest commandment?"

"You shall love the Lord your God with heart and soul and mind. You shall love your neighbor as you love yourself."

They have questioned him, but they still haven't caught him out. His answer may be too clever, but it's not wrong. They may not be ready to give him a doctorate, but they can't flunk him yet, either. There are no grounds to let him go.

Then Jesus gives them the grounds, of course. Give any too-clever graduate student time and opportunity, and odds are there will be some mistake. In this case Jesus' student etiquette goes all awry. "I'll question you," he says to the faculty.

"Who does he think he is?" they mumble, to themselves.

"Who do you think I am?" he asks, as if guessing their thoughts.

He puts it in the third person, but they know his question is about himself all right. "Who do you think I am? Do you think I'm David's son?"

They hem and haw. That may be giving him too much. If Jesus is King David's son, he can be a leader of his people, a great human being.

Jesus makes the question even harder. "Calling me David's son doesn't claim too much for me," says Jesus. "Calling me David's son claims too little."

Then Jesus constructs or deconstructs a text and completely baffles them. He quotes a psalm, and says that in this psalm King David looks ahead and calls Jesus his own Lord. "That's who I am," says Jesus. "Not just a great human leader. I am God's agent, David's Lord, your Lord."

The exam is over. The examiners storm angrily from the seminar room. He has turned the tables altogether. They came to question him. He stayed to question them. Then he answers his own question. He not only says he's got the answer, he says he IS the answer.

The departmental orthodoxy is overturned. All usual expectations are undone. Jesus said: "Love the Lord with heart and soul and mind." That's not so bad, but then Jesus has gone on. "I reveal the Lord you are to love," he says. "I am Immanuel, God with you."

"Come unto me, all you who labor and are heavy laden, and I will give you rest. Take my yoke upon you and learn of me, for I am gentle and lowly of heart, and you shall find rest for your soul."

The God whose love makes possible our loves comes close in this man, this student, this fellow failing this exam.

Jesus says, "Love your neighbor as you love yourself." That's not too bad, but then Jesus has gone on. "I am the one who shows you your neighbor. You are called to love me in your neighbor. Whenever you do it to one of the least of these my brothers and sisters, you do it to me."

"Love God and love your neighbor," says Jesus, and his examiners don't mind. "Love God in me and me in your neighbor," says Jesus, and suddenly it's all wrong, all odd, all puzzling. The examiners are put to the test. We are put to the test. Who is this man? What shall we do with him?

V

Four hundred and seventy-three years ago this week, Martin Luther started the Protestant Reformation, and these days he also nourishes the Catholic one.

Luther went looking for a God who is gracious and for a neighbor to serve. In Christ he found God's lovingkindness, and through Christ he was directed to his neighbor's need. Though he was proud enough of his own doctorate, he had come to see that only one person ever passed the exam that really counted and gained one inestimably high degree.

"We must away with invalid doctors," Luther wrote, "and hold fast the doctor God has validated. God designated Christ our doctor and teacher, who is the light of the world, and whose commission is—to lead us to himself."

Luther could put it more poetically:

> Did we in our own strength confide,
> Our striving would be losing.
> Were not the right man on our side,
> That man of God's own choosing.
> Dost ask who that may be?
> Christ Jesus, it is he.
> The lord of Hosts his name,
> From age to age the same,
> And he must win the battle.

To Christ be thanks and praise.
Amen.

October 11, 1991 ·
Yale Divinity School ·
Mark 2:1-12

I

"Which is easier, to say to the paralytic, 'Your sins are forgiven,' or to say, 'Stand up and take your mat and walk'?"

I don't know.

I used to know which was easier, but I don't know any longer.

Of course, Mark must not get Jesus quite right here. At the most obvious level it's exceedingly simple to SAY either of these things. It's easy to say, "Your sins are forgiven," and it's easy to say, "Stand up and take your mat and walk." What's hard is to make the words effective, to make them count.

I am also fairly sure what Mark thinks is the right answer to Jesus' question. For Mark, healing is a fine gift but a modest one. Forgiveness, however, that is a power astonishing beyond belief.

Certainly it's beyond the belief of the scribes. They accuse Jesus of blasphemy. "Who can forgive sins but God alone?" they ask. A classic case of Markan irony. They've got it right for the wrong reasons. God alone DOES forgive sins. In Jesus Christ, God forgives sins.

For Mark, nothing could be harder, or more true.

But now, in this century, in this place, which is easier to say effectively—"Your sins are forgiven" or, "Stand, take up your mat and walk"?

The early form critics, looking for *Sitz im Leben* under every pericope, found one here. They suggest that this story was told so that the early church could validate its authority to forgive sins and transgressions, in Jesus' name.

Hard though it may be, that is the authority that the church has taken on, powerfully, effectively. Many of us have stood at the pulpit or the table and said to our people: "In the name of Jesus Christ, you are forgiven." And we have said it truly, effectively. It was so.

All of us have sat in the pews after confession, waiting for the word that grants us mercy. "In the name of Jesus Christ you are forgiven," and we ARE forgiven. Our sins are loosed on earth and loosed in heaven. It is so.

In the drama of our iniquity, there is often a happy ending: "Your sins are forgiven."

II

"Which is easier, to say to the paralytic, 'Your sins are forgiven,' or to say, 'Stand up and take your mat and walk'?"

I know one paralytic well. Though my prayers and the prayers of many other Christians have been raised to God that he might walk again, I am almost certain that he won't. The spinal cord is smashed. The connections will not reconnect. It is hard to say, "Stand up and walk," because it will not accomplish anything to say those words.

His name is David, and he used to be the meanest squash player alive, and about the most active husband and father. That family was always DOING things—playing or running or tackling. They were even building their own house.

One night in the rain David climbed up on the roof of the unfinished house to cover a hole with a tarp. He slipped and fell onto the cement below. Paralyzed. Quadriplegic.

He has been graced and prayed into courage. He has found remarkable resources. Unlike the man in our story, no one has to carry David around. He uses his elbows to drive the wheelchair to the lift that raises him into the van he also drives.

He is a marvel of courage sustained by marvels of technology.

He would give it all up just once more to toss a ball to his children or to run along the beach.

It may not be easy to say, "Your sins are forgiven," but it is effective. To say to David, "Get up and walk"—that would be its own kind of blasphemy.

Or Sally, whose body works all right but whose mind is slipping toward paralysis. When she was younger Sally's greatest pleasure was to sing for fun, for friends. She sounded a little like sly Bette Midler, before Midler turned soapy and serious.

A few years ago something started going wrong with Sally's memory. Connections missed. It might be that the problem would have cleared up in time, but an eager doctor thought he should explore, and the instrument slipped, ever so slightly, and since then the connections have got worse and worse. Sally does not sing any more.

Those who love her have tried to pray and urge and exhort that splendid spirit back from paralysis, but we've discovered that it's the hardest thing in the world to say: "Come on. Get up. Sing."

III

"Which is easier, to say to the paralytic, 'Your sins are forgiven,' or to say, 'Stand up and take your mat and walk'? But so that you may know that the Son of Man has authority on earth to forgive sins"—he said to the paralytic, "I say to you, stand up, and take your mat, and go home." And the man stood up.

It doesn't help that it looks as though Mark makes some connection here between iniquity and illness, God visiting this man's sins on his immobile body. So the healed body proves that the sins are forgiven. Cause and effect.

To be sure, my friend David got a little careless before he slipped from his roof. But if the wages of a little carelessness were paralysis, how many of us would have been able to walk to Chapel this morning?

To be sure, Sally's surgeon probably should have waited, and the scalpel did slip, but if we helpers always wait until we are sure, our souls will all be paralyzed.

The truth is, we know full well that it's hard to make any clear connection between iniquity and disaster or between forgiveness and health. Forgiven, people still ride in wheelchairs. Forgiven, people watch their memories slip away.

More than that, in the long run perhaps the happy ending of this morning's brief story doesn't help. At twenty-five I loved it: sins forgiven, paralytic healed, the crowd cheers, everyone lives happily ever after. At fifty I'm glad that Mark's story goes on. At fifty I'm glad that this little story is part of a larger story, a Gospel.

Mark's Gospel does seem to start out cheerfully enough. Jesus in his own home. Forgiving sins. Healing the paralytic.

The story ends much more ambiguously. Jesus in a borrowed room in somebody else's house, serving supper.

The healer who made the broken paralytic whole picks up a loaf and says, "This is my body." Then he breaks the loaf, breaks himself.

He picks up a cup and says: "This is my blood. This is a promise for many. The promise is that one day you will drink with me—new—in the Kingdom of God."

Then he goes out and is broken: tied down to a cross like the paralytic to the bed, tied down through no fault of his own, broken for no sin of his own.

Three days later (Mark is so reticent here), three days later, an empty tomb, and silence, and ambiguity and hope.

We need the longer story. It is not enough for us any more that the healer says to the paralytic, "Your sins are forgiven. Get up. Take up your mat and walk."

We need the longer story, where the healer, too, is broken— and shares our brokenness.

We need the promise and the ambiguity and the hope which point to a Kingdom we do not yet see and to a meal we only anticipate, where the loaf will be whole again, and the wine will be shared, just as Jesus promised.

A meal that David will run to enjoy, and where Sally will join in singing the final hymn—every note, every word.

We need the longer story, not the quick fix and happy shout, but the Gospel, which moves toward silence, and brokenness, and hope.

Like David's story, and Sally's story, and your story. And the world's story, too.

Amen.

November 21, 1991 ·
Yale Divinity School ·
Matthew 28:16-20

*The following sermon derives from a series of three sermons
in Marquand Chapel given by three different Divinity
School faculty members, of which Dean Bartlett was one.
The topic for the three sermons was to be Jesus' significance
for the world today.*

I

The first clue that I might find my vocation as a professor of
preaching came in high school when I entered a public speaking
contest sponsored by the Lions Club. The set theme for the contest
was "Community Service: A Way of Life." I took as the center of
my address one of my adolescent heroes, Albert Schweitzer. I
paid particular attention to his sacrificial decision to give his life
to medical service in Africa.

It was not the first time or the last that Christian heroism had
been tailored to meet the more modest aspirations of the Lions
Club, but for me the contest brought several rewards. When it
was over I had a large trophy and a permanent addiction to the
sound of my own voice. Equally important, I had a scholarship to
help make possible my first year in college.

It was in college that I learned more about my hero as a
biblical scholar. Schweitzer, as you all know, had surveyed the

19th century discussions of the historical Jesus. He discovered that scholars searching for Jesus looked down a deep well. At the bottom of the well they thought they saw Jesus, but what they really saw was only their own reflection.

To shift the image, Schweitzer himself looked for the historical Jesus through a telescope, though one might say he looked through the wrong end. The historical Jesus receded exceedingly far into the mists of Jewish apocalypticism. Especially using Matthew's Gospel, Schweitzer found or reconstructed a Jesus so far from the concerns of 20th century liberal German scholarship that there was finally not much point in studying him. One could only follow him—so off to Africa.

As with most adolescent heroes, by this time Schweitzer was also receding into the mists of my ambivalence, and my distance from him was only increased by the wisdom of new mentors discovered when I came to study at Yale Divinity School.

Karl Barth, who was not always respectful of those with whom he disagreed, was unfailingly respectful of Schweitzer, but he disagreed nonetheless. Barth thought that Schweitzer's mystical response to Jesus wandered perilously close to pantheism. Political theologians reminded me that in Schweitzer's heroic trip to Africa there was more than a hint of imperialistic *noblesse oblige*. Perhaps most important, biblical scholars made me rethink the way Schweitzer treated the Gospels.

A paradigm of my biblical scholarly heroes was and is Amos Niven Wilder, who is both a scholar and a poet—from my bias as rich a mix as anyone dare wish. Well ahead of his time, Wilder tried to bring the insights of literary criticism to bear on the Gospels. Wilder reminded us that what we have in Matthew's Gospel, for example, is not so much the record of Schweitzer's odd apocalyptic historical Jesus as Matthew's own poetical shaping of the stories about Jesus. The stories are rooted in history, but the Gospel says what Matthew wants to say. It was the stories, shaped into Gospel, more than the elusive facts about Jesus that could shape our faith.

II

Influenced by Wilder and his like to this day, when I was assigned the task of talking about the ongoing significance of Jesus Christ for today I tried to find a place in the New Testament where a Gospel itself addresses that question. I came to Matthew's Gospel, arguably the most carefully shaped of the Gospels. In Matthew's Gospel I turned to the place where the evangelist and poet explicitly shapes his story toward our question: "Who is Jesus Christ for the generation that outlives the apostles and evangelists? Who is Jesus Christ for each today?"

The first claim the Risen Jesus makes in our passage affirms his significance; he bears witness to himself. "All authority in heaven and on earth has been given to me."

Intellectually I acknowledge the centrality of that claim both for Matthew's Gospel and for Christian faith from that day until this: "All authority."

Existentially what makes me nervous about this undoubted truth is that humanly easy slip from Christ's authority to our authoritarianism.

Those of you who aren't Baptists may not have such memories, but in the church camps of my youth we regularly sang a chorus which starts out all right:

"Now I belong to Jesus."

But the chorus immediately slips into disaster:

"Now I belong to Jesus,

Jesus belongs to me."

Put it another way. About ten years ago our highways were edified by the ubiquitous bumper stickers that showed an index finger pointed heavenward. The stickers carried only these words: "One Way!" We knew that the subtext, assumed but never spoken, was also there: "One way, and I know just what it is." Or, "One way, and it's my way."

We need Christ as God's total gift without spiritual totalitarianism. We need Christ's triumph without Christian triumphalism. We need to stand in awe before the claim, "All authority is given to me," but we do not want to stand there very long.

The one who HAS authority will not let us stand there very long. This is not a claim about metaphysics but about discipleship: "Go therefore."

That surely is what Bonhoeffer discovered, who looked at Matthew as seriously as Schweitzer and Wilder, but somewhat differently. Bonhoeffer discovered that the one who has authority to send us forth to discipleship—that we will not really know him until we serve him; that at the limit of our faithfulness stands the possibility that we will have to join in the sufferings of God at the hands of a godless world.

I know it's stretching the text, but I do wonder whether Jesus' command to "Go" isn't in part his response to that odd feature of Matthew's passage. "The disciples worshipped him, but some doubted." Jesus doesn't stop to argue them out of doubt; he just says, "Go."

Then he says, "And remember, I am with you always, to the end of the age."

Amos Wilder had it right. Matthew is a poet or Jesus is a poet, or both. See how nicely Matthew rounds the Gospel out. In the beginning, before the birth, the word to Joseph: "They will call him Emmanuel, God with us." At the end, after the resurrection, the word to the disciples: "I am with you always." God with us. Jesus Christ is God over us; but even more, God with us: God with us not so much on the mountain of contemplation or in the assurances of dogmatics but in the costly discipleship which may have its doubts but which, by God, does keep on going. Serving. Witnessing.

III

I tried to find some way to wrap it up when providentially a friend of mine sent me a book of essays to review. The essays are by Amos Niven Wilder. The most interesting essay is an appreciation of Albert Schweitzer, whose contribution to New Testament studies Wilder says we must learn to value again.

So Wilder drove me back to Schweitzer, and there I found the words I had underlined decades before. Not just exactly what I wanted to say, but more than close enough:

"He comes to us as One unknown . . . as of old, by the lakeside, he came to those who knew Him not. He speaks to us the same word, 'Follow thou me!' and sets us to the tasks which He has to fulfill for our time. He commands, and to those who obey Him, whether they be wise or simple, He will reveal himself in the toils, the conflicts, the sufferings which they shall pass through in His fellowship, and, as an ineffable mystery, they shall learn in their own experiences, who He is."

Amen.

April 17, 1992 ·
Battell Chapel ·
Luke 23, Isaiah 53

Good Friday was the occasion of this sermon, preached for
The Church of Christ in Yale.

I

The climax of Luke's Gospel seems so anticlimactic.

At the end of Mark's Gospel, after Jesus has cried his terrible cry—"My God, my God, why have you abandoned me"—the centurion looks up at the cross in astonishment and faith: "Surely this was the Son of God."

In Matthew's Gospel not only the cry but signs from heaven and portents on earth, and the centurion looks up and confesses: "Surely this was the Son of God."

In Luke's Gospel, at the very end of the same scene, Jesus breathing his last, the centurion looks at Christ on the cross and says: "Surely this man was innocent."

Innocent. From the grandeur of faith to the formulas of a Perry Mason movie. Innocent, of course he's innocent. Go on. Say more.

Yet maybe more than we admit, innocence is our problem and our puzzle. We think we know how the story deals with sin and guilt and judgment and redemption, but how does the Gospel deal with innocence?

Not only Jesus' innocent suffering but the innocent suffering of people we love. Lee and Jeff Irish and their parents were vacationing in Italy when suddenly, almost instantly, Lee contracted meningitis and died within hours.

Jeff, who was twelve, wrote a poem about the death of his 13-year-old brother:

> I looked up to him,
> I twelve, and he a boy thirteen,
> I remember very well looking up and there he was with
>   the train window down,
> His head a little ways out with the wind blowing.
> He was my brother, my only brother.
> My brother who I could talk to,
> One who could eat as no one else.
> He died because he happened to breathe in some bacteria
> That probably can only be seen under some special
>   microscope.
> I guess all I can say is that I loved him and needed him
> And that I don't understand.

Luke knew about that, about those whom we love and who die when we most need them, and whose death or departure or suffering or pain we will never even pretend to understand.

Luke tells Jesus' story here, and then in the second volume of his book Luke tells Stephen's story, not God's only begotten son but God's own child, killed for no reason except that he kept faith in a faithless time.

Luke tells Stephen's story in such a way that it sounds like Jesus' story—courage, faith, innocence—and I think he's saying to those who loved Stephen and needed him: sometimes there is suffering and loss and death that is innocent. And though we cannot explain that or take that away, we can look at the cross and see him there, too, God's own son, God's own beloved; also suffering, altogether innocent.

II

Our Gospel affirms that there is such a thing as undeserved suffering—innocent suffering. But it pushes us beyond that, too. Maybe innocence and guilt are not the most helpful categories when it comes to thinking about suffering. Maybe there is a danger in puzzling too much about innocence.

The danger is that we begin to make distinctions between which suffering is deserved and undeserved, or we chart it out: very innocent death, somewhat innocent, guilty . . .

Have you been following the story of the death of Cindy Marie Beaudoin? She died in the Gulf War. First her parents were told she had tripped a mine while defending a convoy; innocent death, heroic death. Then another phone call: we got it wrong, perhaps she had foolishly picked up live ammunition after the fighting was done. We've changed the cause of death; not so innocent after all.

You get the picture of some person whose job it is to put the deaths into the proper files: heroic, innocent, foolish, negligent, guilty.

We may never know exactly what happened, but whatever happened Cindy Marie Beaudoin was in her country's service, far from home. And our categories may serve only to confuse the pain, the loss, the hope of which those who love her pray.

A kind of implicit labeling goes on around the issue of AIDS. Innocent victims and not-so-innocent victims.

Kimberly Bergalis got AIDS from the dentist. Innocent, tragic.

Arthur Ashe got AIDS from a blood transfusion. Innocent, tragic.

Then, for those who make lists the lists sometimes get confusing. What counts as sin, and how much sin is enough sin to deserve this?

But of course there aren't two viruses, AIDS innocent and AIDS guilty. There's just AIDS. I've seen a lot of people dying from AIDS. Not one deserved it.

Or, the shootings in our communities. We can't make sense of it, of course, so we try to get some control by deciding what kids were caught up in the drug traffic and had it coming, and what kids were innocent passersby.

The drug traffic is awful, evil, killing, but every kid caught in it was once an innocent bystander; some death took instantly, and some it hooked and conned and seduced for a long, long time.

And every death is still a death, and every dead kid is still a victim, and while we have every right to hate what happens to our kids we pray not to let hate win.

And our desire to find good deaths and bad deaths, innocent and guilty is in part our understandable attempt to put some handles on the stuff we apparently cannot control: disease, suffering, death.

The truth is that while guilt and innocence are very useful categories in dealing with the law and may be useful categories in thinking about ethics, they are not very useful categories in thinking about suffering.

Innocent and guilty alike (and most of us are innocent and guilty alike), we get caught in pain disproportionate to our fault, and sorrow inexplicable by our guilt. And it is not a valid explanation of human pain to say that God likes to play "Gotcha."

III

Luke knows that too, Jesus on the cross, this innocent man, looks ahead to Stephen the innocent martyr whose death can be so frightening; but he also speaks to the thief there beside him on the cross, penitent at last after a life of robbery or banditry or guerilla warfare, we're not quite sure which. The criminal tries to do it our way, with the best of intentions. When his friend rails at Jesus, the thief replies: "Do you not fear God, since you are under the same sentence of condemnation? And we have been condemned justly, for we are getting what we deserve for our deeds, but this man has done nothing wrong."

Jesus hears the distinction between guilt and innocence; his silence neither affirms it or denies it; he accepts it, he transcends it.

"Jesus!" says the thief, "Remember me when you come into your kingdom." Jesus replies: "Truly I tell you, today, you will be with me in Paradise."

"Lord Jesus, receive my spirit," Stephen will cry, and in his vision see the Lord reach out to welcome him.

Guilt on the one side, innocence on the other; acknowledged, redeemed, transcended.

That is the gift we need. Because sometimes the innocent suffer, and sometimes the guilty suffer, but mostly the suffering we know is our own suffering—and the suffering of people we love. And we're not as good as we want to be or as bad as we might be, and whatever our suffering is about it's NOT mostly about rewards and punishment because the God who lets rain fall on the just and the unjust lets death and devastation fall there too.

Whatever redemption includes, it needs to find room to deal both with innocence and with guilt, or it will not deal with us at all.

IV

Who has believed what we have seen? And to whom has the arm of the Lord been revealed? What happens on this day on this cross, for the redemption of Stephen in his innocence and the thief in his guilt and most of us caught in between?

We cannot tell it, because it is mystery; we cannot avoid it, because it is mystery.

The book *Lest Innocent Blood Be Shed*, is subtitled: *The Story of the Village of Le Chambon and How Goodness Happened There.*

A goodness happened in Le Chambon in large measure because the village pastor Andrew Trocmé inspired his people to shelter, hide and aid Jews in their escape from the cruelties of the pro-Nazi regime.

Yet the heroic story moves to a terrifying climax: Trocmé who has given his life to protecting others, cannot protect himself. In a terrible calculation or miscalculation, Trocmé's beloved son Jean-Pierre is hanged.

Something changed in Trocmé from that day; the suffering outside himself he now took into himself. From then on, he wrote, his heart silently bled underneath, while he himself bore a scar, like a tree.

Here is the news of the Gospel; this day something has changed in God; in Calvary the suffering outside Godself, God has taken in.

From now on God bears our suffering like a scar, like a tree. Amen.

May 25, 1992 ·
Yale Divinity School ·
Deuteronomy 8:1-20,
John 6:52-71

At the Commencement exercises in May each year, the Divinity School faculty and graduating class share a final Eucharist service together in Marquand Chapel before the students graduate and take their leave. This sermon is from the Commencement Eucharist service of 1992.

I

"Many of his disciples turned back and no longer went with him. So Jesus asked the twelve: 'Do you also want to go away?'"

Some days you will. It may be hard to believe this morning, full of promise and promises, but some days you will want to go away.

You may want to go away when you discover that the challenges to faith raised by your teachers are nothing compared to the challenges raised by your students. You may want to go away when the question of theodicy isn't an abstract question but a small coffin or a young body wasting away or a gentle soul turned sour by old age. You may want to go away when you discover that prayer changes things, but not as many things as you'd wished. You may want to go away if you came to seminary inspired by some mentor and discover that you're not measuring up; or you came to seminary knowing that you'd do better than that example back home and discover that you're doing it pretty much the same.

You may want to go away when you grow weary with well doing; or just weary. You may want to go away when you start out making a joyful noise to the Lord, and then just a joyful noise, and then just noise.

"Do you also want to go away?" Some days you will. Some days you will also want to go away.

II

What will you cling to, when you want to go away? To Christ, of course. But how will you cling to him?

This sixth chapter of John gives oddly contradictory answers. "Unless you eat my flesh and drink my blood," says Jesus, "you will not have eternal life." And then, two breaths later: "The flesh is worth nothing. My words are Spirit. My words are life."

What is this—a Baptist sermon edited by some Catholic? Some kind of happy synthesis or a hopeless contradiction? A paradox, I suppose; a mystery; a blessed confusion.

The word gives life. "Will you also go away from me?" Jesus asks the twelve. Peter, often there with the right answer, responds: "Lord, to whom shall we go? For you have the words of eternal life."

When you want to go away, come back to the words.

Come back to the words of Scripture. Parsed and puzzled by your courses here, but we hope not dissected or vivisected. Come back to the old old stories that can shape your stories, and the psalms that can shape your prayers and the commands that can lead you through the wilderness at least to the very edge of the Promised Land.

Come back to the words of sermons, of course. Many of you preach better sermons than you usually hear. Do not wear out or burn out or cop out. Find preachers who will feed your own soul. Preach sermons that will speak to your own deepest longings, and others will be touched.

Come back to the words that define you. To those words spoken to us: "In the name of Jesus Christ I declare that your sins are forgiven." To the words spoken by us: "I believe in the Father Almighty, Maker of heaven and earth, and in Jesus Christ his only Son our Lord." Above all come back to the words spoken for us: "I baptize you in the name of the Father and of the Son and of the Holy Spirit." Vows sealed on earth and in heaven, the truest thing about you—more true than the name or vocation or denomination or degree. Come back to that.

"Lord, to whom shall we go? You have the words of eternal life."

III

And then, not just on the other hand, but almost from some other place in God's own heart: "Unless you eat the flesh of the Son of Man and drink his blood, you have no life in you." Word and food together, inseparable like manna and Torah in the wilderness.

When you want to go away, cling to Christ's flesh.

Walker Percy died a few months ago. He wrote a number of novels where he grumbled at various American heresies. One of his worst fears was what he called "angelism"—really I think it was his reading of Protestantism, long on words and short on flesh.

The hero of one of Percy's novels, not coincidentally named Thomas More, leaves his Protestant wife each Sunday morning and heads off to Mass. More describes one of his typical Sunday mornings: "Here comes the bemused priest with his cup. What am I doing here? says his dazed expression. He announces the turkey raffle and Wednesday bingo and preaches the Gospel and feeds me Christ.

"I drive back to Doris.

"She opens one eye, 'My God, what is it that you do in church?'

"What she didn't understand, she being spiritual and seeing religion as spirit, was that it took religion to save me from the spirit world, that it took nothing less than driving the interstate and eating Christ himself to make me mortal man again and let me inhabit my own flesh and love her in the morning."

When you want to go away, hang on to Christ's flesh in the sacrament. It does avail to make us human, his humanity. His incarnation lets us fully inhabit our own flesh, lest we drift off to pure spirit or total theological abstraction. When you are tempted to go away—bread's chewiness, wine's tang can anchor you to earth, and to Christ, too.

And more than that. Christ' flesh is not only the body on the table, it's the body around the table. The brothers and sisters, pastors, priests, ministers of music, Christian educators, unbending bishops, fussy children, befuddled adolescents, pinchpenny treasurers, you, me. It's no coincidence that before he said the words of institution Walker Percy's priest announced the turkey raffle and the bingo game. It goes together.

When you are tempted to run from Christ you will be tempted first of all to run from Christ's people to some pure piety of word and sacrament. But the good news and the hard news are the same. The word is spoken among Christ's people, the church. And the sacraments are celebrated there as well. The odd, fleshy, and recalcitrant church, with room for the most intractable, befuddled, and doubting souls: with room, therefore, for you and me.

"Do you also want to go away?" our Lord asks. "Lord," says Peter, quick as always with a heartwarming answer: "To whom can we go? For you have the words of eternal life."

But a few weeks later, months at most, off he goes. Turns tail and runs to save his hide from the terror of following the Word of Life.

Christ seeks him out of course, there in that twenty-first chapter of this Gospel of John. "Run away if you will, Peter. But I will not let you go."

Christ seeks him out of course, finds him there on the beach, and gives him what Christ always gives.

A meal.

A word.

A people: "Simon, son of John, do you love me?"

"Lord, you know I love you."

"Feed my sheep."

Will we want to go away? Of course we will. Time after time after time. And sometimes we'll even pack our bags and start the trip.

> Christ will not let us go
> but turns to us
> in word
> and sacrament,
> and—most amazing—church,
> He comes to us, again, again, again.

Amen.

March 4, 1993 ·
Duke Divinity School ·
Jeremiah 9:23-24,
Matthew 20:1-16

Following is the only sermon of the collection not preached at Yale, from one of Dean Bartlett's visits to Duke Divinity School in North Carolina. This sermon was entitled "The Vineyard."

Thus says the Lord, "Do not let the wise boast in their wisdom, do not let the mighty boast in their might, do not let the wealthy boast in their wealth; but let those who boast boast in this, that they understand and know me, that I am the Lord. I act with steadfast love, justice, and righteousness in the earth, for in these things I delight, says the Lord."

I

All of us came to the vineyard early.

All of us are eldest children, if not biologically then psychologically. We work hard to please our parents, our professors, our bishops or our congregations.

We are the first ones up in the morning, and we do our share of family chores and more. We are responsible, and while our younger siblings—if not biologically then psychologically—while our younger siblings party well past curfew or skip their daily jobs, we're always home fifteen minutes early. We do OUR jobs and volunteer for more. (We are a little jealous that our younger brothers and sisters get as much love as we do—at less cost.)

All of us came to the vineyard early, and stay at the library late. We're there to unlock the sanctuary door on Sunday and to clean up after coffee hour. We write twenty page papers when ten pages would do, and we buy all the books on the suggested reading list, even if we don't quite finish reading all of them.

Taking God with utter seriousness we give our lives to "fulltime Christian service" or to "set apart ministry." Or we prepare to teach religion. Partly because religion interests us; partly because that discipline meets our own need to ask ultimate questions in a proximate age.

We are a little jealous that part time Christians who are not so set apart sometimes take their faith more lightly, or at least more joyfully than we. We are a little envious of those colleagues in other disciplines who think that proximate questions will do just fine.

All of us came to the vineyard early. We believe in God's amazing grace and work extremely hard to understand what we believe. To cite authorities for grace and to get the footnotes on God's mercy right.

All of us came to the vineyard early. We have a secret theological hope that supererogation may yet count for something and Christian perfection is perfectly appealing.

To show how early we got here, how long we have been working, we take on titles: Reverend, Doctor, Professor. Labels that separate us from those other workers who came sneaking in by sheer luck at the final roll call, just before the gates slammed shut.

All of us came to the vineyard early, or we wouldn't be here in this earnest, hard-driven place. We are glad for God's great goodness to us and a little bit annoyed that so many people seem to know that goodness with less work than we.

We are sure that our extra effort must be worth it.

But we're not sure why.

II

All of us came to the vineyard late.

All of us sneaked in just in the nick of time. Just before curfew, or fifteen minutes after, praying no one would know.

Not one of us lived up to our parents' expectations or our mentors' expectations or God's apparent expectations—or our own.

All of us came to the vineyard late. We came to ourselves and dashed back from the Far Country just two minutes before we would have gone so far that there would be no turning back. All of us wasted our substance in riotous living or hoarded our substance in compulsive living until we feared that we'd have nothing left to give.

All of us came to the vineyard late. We whip off a pretty good paper at the last minute, while our roommate turns in that masterpiece she finished three days early. Friday we start work on Sunday's sermon while that Presbyterian down the street has planned his sermon outlines for the next two years.

All of us came to the vineyard late, slipping a slender tome to the Dean just before the tenure review, put there on the shelf beside the twelve-volume study of Syriac Christianity our colleague finished writing just past puberty.

All of us came to the vineyard late. Perhaps after a career went sour or a marriage went bust. All of us came to the vineyard late, wondering whether there was any work for those of us for whom so much had NOT worked out.

All of us came to the vineyard late for reasons that aren't anybody's business but God's business and our own—since if the vineyard owner marked iniquity, then who would stand? Or stand in line waiting for wages, either one?

"Are you envious because I am generous?" the owner asks. But how can we not be envious?

All of us came to the vineyard late, or we would not be here at all. Waiting in line, shuffling our feet, holding out unsteady hands, receiving wages—

Which are not wages after all, but gift, sheer gift, sheer mercy
for those who got here early and for those who got here late

> waiting in line, shuffling our feet, holding out unsteady hands,
> receiving gifts and mercy
> blood and body
> bread and wine.

To Christ be thanks and praise. Amen.

September 2, 1993 · Yale Divinity School · Isaiah 55, Romans 1:8-17

I

"I am not ashamed of the Gospel," says the apostle, introducing himself to a bunch of strangers in Rome.

Well I may not be ashamed of the Gospel, but I do get embarrassed. Especially around strangers.

"Where do you teach?" ask faculty colleagues from the Faculty of Arts and Sciences. "At the Divinity School," I say softly. "What do you teach?" "Preaching," I mumble. "What?" "Preaching," I mumble.

Or riding on an airplane, even if I'm reading a book on theology or biblical studies I sneak it inside a copy of *Newsweek* or *The New Yorker*. Desperately hoping to avoid those awful conversations.

"I see that you're reading a book on religion. Are you a preacher?" "Yes," I mumble. Or, "No, I teach." Hoping they won't say more.

But they do say more. "I hate religion. Ever since my parents made me go to Sunday School."

Or: "I used to be more religious, and I'm sorry I'm not any more."

Or: "Well, I have a problem I've been wanting to talk over with someone, and since you're a preacher . . ."

Or: "Well, I just read an article somewhere that proved that Jesus was illegitimate, or a zealot, or an invention of St. Paul . . ."

I'm not ashamed of the Gospel, maybe not even embarrassed by the Gospel, but a little embarrassed about working for the Gospel, about being a professional proclaimer.

I don't like to intrude on other people's space, geographically or religiously. I don't stick my elbow on the armrest between the seats on the airplane, or stick my religion out there for all to see.

No bumper stickers and no license plates saying: Jesus Loves U. Or "Connecticut, the Constitution State, John 3:16."

Modest commitment. Decorous devotion.

II

"I am not ashamed of the Gospel," says the apostle, "because it is the power of God." And perhaps it's the power that we tend to underestimate, in a Gospel grown conventional and a vocation grown professional. We forget, surrounded by the words we make and the words we hear, that words still have power to shape and change and hurt and heal, like seed to the sower or bread to the eater.

Did you hear the tributes when Thurgood Marshall died? Sandra Day O'Connor who disagreed with him on a thousand things: "I will miss sitting down with Thurgood and listening to him tell the stories that changed the way I see the world."

I am not ashamed of the Gospel, for it is the power of God, the story that changes the way we see the world. More than that: the story that changes the world we see.

III

I am not ashamed of the power of the Gospel to justify the ungodly, Paul says; to make us right with God while we are still sinners.

Last year, Mr. Rogers came to Yale to give a speech. Battell Chapel was packed with eighteen year olds and nineteen year olds and twenty-four year old med students and twenty-two year old budding attorneys.

I think I know why: In a University whose two watchwords ought not to be "Light and Truth" but "Achieve and Compete," in the midst of the stress that strains toward endless evaluation and sufficient accomplishment, hundreds of young women and men came to spend one hour with the man who all those years before used to look each one of them straight in the eye and say in the gentlest of voices: "I like you just the way you are."

Not: I like everything about the way you are.

Not: there is nothing you could do differently.

But: as you are, I like you.

It's only a parable of Paul's Gospel but not a bad parable just the same: "While we were still weak, at the right time, Christ died for the ungodly." God's love for us before our achieving or competing or striving. The power of the Gospel.

IV

I am not ashamed of the power of the Gospel to reconcile those who are divided. "The Gospel is the power of God for salvation to everyone who has faith," says Paul, "to the Jew first and also to the Greek."

I'm persuaded by lots of people that Jews and Greeks weren't getting along all that well in the churches of first century Rome. Fighting about rules and menus at church dinners and who had the right to lead whom . . . all the kind of stuff churchy people still fight about today. But also fighting out of those deep divisions that seem to come with our fallen humanity: my race vs. your race; my social class vs. your social class, or denomination, or sexuality.

The truth is we've twisted Mr. Rogers and further twisted the Gospel of which he is parable: not I like you just the way you are, but I'll like you if the way you are is just like me.

Have you heard some of those stories Thurgood Marshall told Sandra Day O'Connor? Stories of exclusion and derision,

doors locked, access denied. Stories that change the way we see
the world; that help us see the power of sin so that we can affirm
the power of reconciling grace, of the cross where Christ's
outstretched arms must reach wide enough to encompass all those
people we find so difficult to know or understand, or love. "I am
not ashamed of the Gospel for it is the power of God for faithful
Jews and faithful Greeks."

Or as he puts it even more powerfully elsewhere: "There is
no longer Jew or Greek; there is no longer slave or free; there is
no longer male or female; for all of you are one in Christ Jesus."

V

I am not ashamed of the Gospel; it is the power of God for
salvation. For in it the righteousness of God is revealed to everyone
who has faith; as it is written, "The one who is righteous will live
by faith."

The power of the Gospel to assure us of the love of God for
each of us; the power of the Gospel to work love in us toward one
another. That power received, accepted, celebrated—in faith.
Faith in the God who does love us, just the way we are; faith in
the God who does work reconciliation in the world, for folk who
are pretty much the way we are and for folk who are pretty much
entirely different. Faith in the power of God's Gospel to work for
good in the midst of all the stuff that drags us down and all the
stuff that wounds the world.

Frederick Buechner's book *Telling Secrets* tells of his own
pain and frustration in the face of his daughter's anorexia, when
he wanted to be God and change everything and discovered he
was just human and couldn't change much at all. He was driving
one day through his state of Vermont and stopped at a rest stop,
worn out by worry and frustration, and his eyes wandering he
noticed a car driving by on the highway and noticed, too, the
vanity license plate which for once was not vanity but testimony:
"TRUST" it said. Just "TRUST." Which for that day was Gospel

and power and the word sufficient to get Buechner going again, and hoping again, too.

Hear the Apostle: The Gospel is the power of God through faith for faith, as it is written: (and Paul quotes Habakkuk): "The one who is righteous will live by faith."

So Buechner searching his brain and scanning the horizon stumbled upon the license plate that got him through.

Truth is I think that Paul, scanning the Bible or searching his brain, found the verse that brought it all together: Habakkuk 2:4. The one who is righteous will live by faith.

You have to admire the trust officer at the bank who took his title and punned on it, and stuck it on a license plate where it became hope and comfort. TRUST.

You have to admire Buechner who took the license plate and turned it into a story that changes the way we see the world.

You have to admire Paul who took Habakkuk 2:4 and stuck it into a letter to the Romans where it became the Gospel.

And what a Gospel. "Trust."

To trust the God who loves us.

To trust the God who reconciles all people and will reconcile the whole creation.

In the light of such a Gospel, who could be embarrassed?

Who could be ashamed?

Amen.

August 14, 1994 ·
Battell Chapel ·
Ephesians 5:6-20

In this sermon, Dean Bartlett refers to the Puritan ancestors, meaning both the founders of Yale and the early Congregationalists. "New Broadway" in this sermon refers to the renovations to Broadway Street in downtown New Haven.

I

Let's face it. It's not easy getting along with new believers. In all their enthusiasm for faith they can sometimes leave the rest of us behind, a little lukewarm, a little skeptical, a little tired.

Even when we ourselves ARE the new believers, we can understand why our old friends find us a little tough to get along with. There IS a kind of tendency to be so sure we're right and that others are wrong; there is a kind of tendency to look down on the pleasures we used to enjoy; to be a little self-righteous when we contrast ourselves with those whose faith isn't so fresh, so new, so real.

Ephesians is written to new believers to remind them what faith looks like. But sometimes faith looks different from the outside than it does from the inside. From the inside we can hear the apostle's enthusiasm: Congratulations you Ephesian Christians; once you were darkness but now you are light.

Their old friends and drinking companions may have had a

different version: Phooey on you Ephesian Christians; once you were delightful but now you are dull.

There is after that old saw written about our Puritan ancestors who founded this University and this denomination. "A Christian is a person who is deathly afraid that someone, somewhere may be having fun."

Well along with all the rest of the New Testament, Ephesians does insist that there's something fundamentally different about living the Christian life: "Once you were darkness but now you are light." And Ephesians even describes the difference in ways that might suggest that the Puritan bashers have got it right about Christian dullness: "Do not act foolishly . . . do not get drunk with wine, for that is debauchery."

It does sound anti-joy; but it isn't meant to sound anti-joy. It's meant to sound the note of deeper joy; sober intoxication.

The mark of the Christian life, of the light in which Christians live is NOT dullness or propriety or self-righteousness. The mark of the Christian life is, of all things: music. And especially hymns. "Do not get drunk with wine for that is debauchery," says the apostle, "but be filled with the Spirit, as you sing psalms and hymns and spiritual songs among yourselves, singing and making melody to the Lord in your hearts, giving thanks to God the Father at all times and for everything in the name of our Lord Jesus Christ."

II

Once you were darkness but now you are light. Once you sang drinking songs but now you sing hymns. Try a story to see if we can get at what Ephesians means about the difference between the life of faith and life before faith.

It was one of those astonishing New Haven days when the humidity lifts and the sky is absolutely clear blue with white clouds and first flowers blooming and exams over and vacations looming and sabbaticals beginning and lunch break for the construction workers trying to give us a New Broadway. I'm

walking along toward Sterling Library and, touched by the sheer
beauty of the day, venture an unusual friendly smile at a stranger
walking in the other direction. "Isn't it a beautiful day," he said.
"It is," I allowed. Then, as he walked on past: "Makes you proud
to be an American."

A little off, I thought, that response. But not entirely off. Struck
with beauty or touched by love or opened to a new idea, it's not
quite enough to say: what luck. Or that's the way it goes. Maybe
part of the human condition is occasionally or frequently to be
astonished by gratitude. And we need to put that gratitude
somewhere, thank something: "It makes you proud to be an
American."

e.e. cummings, the poet, always struggling toward faith, must
have seen a similar New England day and found another place
to focus gratitude:

> i thank You God for most this amazing day:
> for the leaping greenly spirits of trees
> and a blue true dream of sky; and for everything
> which is natural which is infinite which is yes

Now it may be obvious to you that I started working on this
sermon on one of those blue true dream of sky days before today's
dark and thunder; but surely Christians know how to praise God
for rain as well as for sunshine. Indeed my one modest suggestion
for our bulletin is that we stop saying that Coffee Hour will be
outside if it's nice and inside if it's rainy. Better: outside if it's
nice and clear and inside if it's nice and rainy. Ephesians says it
unmistakably: "Giving thanks to God the Father at all times and
for everything in the name of our Lord Jesus Christ."

Once we were darkness but now we are light; once we saw
the beauty of the earth and the glory of the skies and the joy of
human love and said: "What luck!" or "It makes you proud to be
an American". And now we say: "I thank you God for these most
amazing gifts. Thanks!" "Once you were darkness but now you
are light, once you hummed and mumbled and whistled but NOW

you sing psalms and hymns and spiritual songs, giving thanks to God at all times for everything in the name of our Lord Jesus Christ."

Once you were darkness but now you are light; once you saw dimly what now you see brightly. People of faith are not the only people blessed with the goodness of creation or the kindness of others or the love of God. People of faith are those whose eyes are opened and whose lips are opened so that we can sing and say and pray: Thank you God; thanks.

A brief historical footnote: in one of the first records we have about early Christians written by a non-Christian, Pliny writes a letter to his boss the Emperor Trajan and says he's been checking the Christians out and he notices that the main thing they do is get up early in the morning and sing hymns to Christ. "Once you were darkness now you are light. Sing, sing a song."

We do have to go on: being thankful does have consequences. What you sing affects how you live. Seeing the light means walking in the light. And Ephesians is concerned about that, too. "Be careful, then, how you live, not as unwise people but as wise."

Living in the light, living out our hymns, living out our praise means a couple of things for Ephesians—as we look at the larger context of our passage.

One thing being in the light requires, says the Apostle, is fidelity.

He says that if we are the people who sing hymns of thanks to God, then if and when we find a partner with whom to share our lives, what we pledge to that partner is complete fidelity. The claim that we used to be darkness and now are light is bracketed by a discussion of how we live faithfully with the partners God has given us to love.

The language is too patriarchal and authoritarian to please us, but at the heart is the claim that the old vow counts. "Forsaking all others I will cleave only to you."

And of course that is also a standard Christian claim. A little old-fashioned, a little embattled, but right at the heart of the matter.

Notice how Ephesians begins all this talk of living in the

light and singing hymns of praise: "Be imitators of God, and live in love as Christ loved us."

Be imitators of God who in Jesus Christ loves each one of us with perfect fidelity; therefore we are called to live in perfect fidelity to the partner to whom we promise lifelong love.

Turn it around: as we sing praise to the one God to whom we are bound for life and for eternity; so we promise fidelity to the one person to whom we are bound for as long as we live. Monotheism is reflected in monogamy. One faith, one hope, one baptism, one God, one partner.

I served a University parish once where I was often called upon to officiate at weddings for people I didn't know very well. I was perhaps a little too quick to accept the honor, especially since I was called to edit the remarkable variety of marital vows composed by the couples. But one condition always prevailed: no new vows were spoken that implied that marriage left room for multiple partners. Some version of the old words were always spoken: "Forsaking all others cleave only to her," "forsaking all others cleave only to him." I will. I do.

I liked the moment on Bob Newhart's latest show when he's off on a business trip without his wife and an attractive associate is trying to entice him to join her in her hotel room.

"I can see you're playing hard to get."

"I'm not hard," he says, "I'm impossible."

There's a way in which hymns and vows go together; once we were darkness but now we are light. Once we whistled a happy tune to no one in particular and pledged ourselves to no one in particular, too. Now we praise thanks to God and loyalty to our beloved.

Then the larger section of Ephesians makes clear another way in which hymn singing people are supposed to love; another way in which we live out our praise as children of light.

To paraphrase: "Once you stressed your titles and your ranks and your prerogatives but now you are one family in Jesus Christ."

Again it goes back to the hymns we sing: we sing hymns to the God who pledges to us perfect fidelity; and we also sing hymns to the God who Ephesians says is "our master in heaven, who shows no partiality." Doesn't play favorites.

Wayne Meeks, in writing about the early Christian communities, notes that while they borrowed lots of ideas from other institutions around them they didn't borrow the long list of titles and offices and ranks that filled lodges and guild halls.

Notice that even when the early New Testament writings talk about apostles and pastors and elders people usually aren't called apostle or pastor or elder, they're called "sister" or "brother"—family.

When the society of Friends (notice the name: friends) tried to get back to being like the early church they insisted on calling everybody Thou or Thee because You was formal language for people of high rank and Thou was informal language for people of low degree or for children or for your own dear family and friends (like the French *tu* or the German *du*). In the church we're all "Thous."

(Parenthetically it does make me wonder about using titles like Reverend to separate some Christians from others; it can be a way of "you"ing people we ought to "thou.")

Back at that same University church I'll never forget the excitement of the layperson whose rank in the hierarchy of the University was very low indeed who ended up on a church committee with the Chicago equivalent of a Sterling Professor. When my friend dared to ask the Professor a question he began: "Dr. Swift I wonder . . ." and Dr. Swift quickly responded: "My friends call me Charlie."

Once you were darkness, full of professorships and honors and doctorates and degrees high and low and rank and status, but now you are light. Thous, friends, sisters, brothers, Charlie, Maggie, Ann.

See, there is a language to the business of being faithful. There is a way of talking which is also a way of acting.

Who are the people who walk in light?

They sing hymns of praise.

They make absolute vows to the partners they love.

And they call each other by their first names.

Once you were darkness but now you are light.

Once you thanked your lucky stars or whistled a happy tune: now you praise God at all times and for everything in the name of Jesus Christ.

Once you hemmed and hawed and wandered from one relationship to the next: now we pledge exclusive love.

Once we rejoiced in our ranks and titles or humbled ourselves before those who outranked us: now we are brothers and sisters, servants of the only Master, who shows no partiality at all.

Seeing things differently, knowing things differently, singing and making melody to the Lord in our hearts.

> i thank You God for most this amazing day;
> for the leaping greenly spirits of trees and
> a blue true dream of sky; and for everything
> which is natural which is infinite which is yes
>
> i who have died am alive again today,
> and this is the sun's birthday; this is the birth
> day of life and of love and wings; and of the gay
> great happening illimitably earth
>
> how should tasting touching hearing seeing
> breathing any—lifted from the no
> of all nothing—(any) human merely being
> doubt unimaginable You?

"now," the poet says . . .

> now the ears of my ears awake and
> now the eyes of my eyes are opened

Amen we say. Amen.

November 27, 1994 ·
Battell Chapel ·
Luke 21:25-36

Midway through this sermon, Dean Bartlett's words are: "The New Deal may have ended three weeks ago." This sentence refers to the "Contract With America": on November 8, 1994, Republican leaders announced their plans to bring this contract before the House and the Senate. The "Contract With America" included the Personal Responsibility Act, which would deny welfare benefits to mothers having children out of wedlock. Dean Bartlett preached this sermon on the first Sunday of Advent, 1994.

I

As a young pastor, on the first Sunday of Advent, 1974, I walked from the study to the sanctuary, eager and ready for the first Sunday of this high and holy season. On the way I passed Sally Jensen heading for her familiar pew. "Happy Advent!" I cried. "Advent?" she said. "We don't believe in that." Sally and I grew up as Baptists in the years before free churches like the UCC and the American Baptists had caught on to the idea of liturgical renewal.

To put it baldly; in our youth, we had no idea what was going on in the Episcopal, Lutheran and Catholic Churches around us during the season between Thanksgiving and Christmas. Advent? You had to be kidding.

When I was a child, on the Saturday after Thanksgiving, Santa Claus and Mrs. Santa arrived at Lord's store downtown. He was so jolly and she was so sweet that I have always been sure they and they alone were the genuine article.

On the Sunday after Thanksgiving we started singing Christmas carols in church. In perfect keeping with the Christmas music playing in the department stores, only with better arrangements. "O Come, All Ye Faithful," "Joy to the World," and my particular favorite, "Angels We Have Heard On High."

Only much later did I learn that we had it all wrong. Advent is about waiting, not about celebrating. "Joy to the World" is appropriately sung only after 12:01 on Christmas morning. Until then there are advent songs to sing, "O Come, O Come, Immanuel," and "Come Thou Long-Expected Jesus" and—well, the list goes on and on. And the truth is few of them warm the heart like "Angels We Have Heard On High." But by my first year in seminary I was learning to be liturgically correct. I planned worship services for Advent using only Advent hymns.

What the church people hummed on their way home in the car was their own business, of course. What I hummed was mine.

Later yet I was hit with a greater shock. I had got used to Advent as a season of waiting but I assume what we were waiting for was the baby Jesus; manger, shepherd, angels we would hear on high.

When I started using the lectionary, the list of texts assigned for each Sunday of the year by an all-knowing Committee, I was amazed to discover that the Advent texts were often texts like the one we just heard from Luke's Gospel. Texts about the end of the world and Jesus coming on the clouds and signs in heaven and on earth. All the texts I'd tried not to preach about or think about for many, many years.

In turns out that for the liturgically correct, Advent is not just about waiting for Jesus to come in the manger but also about waiting for Jesus to come on the clouds. Not just the first appearance but the second one, the one at the end of history, when "there will be signs in the sun, the moon, and the stars, and on the earth distress among the nations, and Jesus, the Son of Man, will come on the clouds with power and glory."

How I missed my simple naïve roots when we could simply read Isaiah on "unto us a child is born" and sing "Away in a Manger" and get on with it.

II

Advent and The End of the World. Christ coming on the clouds. What can we possibly make of it?

There are people who get rich on The End of the World, of course; predicting all the final signs and then putting away the royalties on the convenient bet that if the world doesn't end as predicted, they'll be financially set while life goes on.

There are the people who go crazy waiting for The End of the World. Waco and Jonestown are terrible reminders that these are texts that promise great hope but sometimes do great harm.

No wonder we want to avoid Scripture that's beloved by charlatans and mad messiahs.

Yet there it is, in three of the Gospels and the book of Acts and most of the letters and the book of Revelation. The claim that history will move toward an end and at the end, Jesus will return, not in the simplicity of a manger stall but in the glory of the clouds and trumpets.

Can we make any sense of it? Put it differently: can we take any hope and comfort from these texts as we move toward Christmas and the stories we know better and understand better, too?

We can admit of course that we know something about endings. It does seem true that nothing goes on forever. We may not have "signs in the sun, the moon, and the stars and on earth distress among nations confused by the roaring of the sea." But we know about endings.

The Cold War ended as we thought it never would. There was a radical shift and the truth is it's hard to know how to make sense of life without the ancient enemy.

The New Deal may have ended three weeks ago. At least that's what some pundits say. It's too early to know whether it was an end or just a shift, but it does seem as though the belief that government has responsibility for compassion is under siege. For those of us who thought we could deliver fair play through our politics, some special hope may have ended or at least grown very small.

Relationships end; the ones we know will end and the ones we count on lasting forever. Somebody walks out or death walks in, or we move away for the best of reasons and there are fewer and fewer phone calls and letters and finally the form letters at Advent time serving sometimes to warm our hearts and sometimes to make us sad for what we've lost, what has ended.

And we end; our lives, every one of us. However deep our faith in resurrection, something very precious comes to a halt. This life, this world which is our world only as long as we're part of it. We can postpone the end for awhile, but we can't avoid it.

What's more, in Luke's Gospel Jesus tells us history will end, too, which shouldn't be a great surprise, the world will be caught up in tragedies we can scarcely imagine and then beyond the tragedies—something more, something blessed, what we wait for at Advent even as we wait for the baby in the manger.

III

Let's try it this way: let's not talk about what the end will look like, since we don't know, not for history or for any one of our histories. Let's talk about how we live in the light of the end. How we live when we know that nothing goes on forever, not even our earthly lives or our earthly history.

For one thing: we live in hope. The main thing about all those signs of the end that Luke tells us about isn't that there'll be earthquakes and floods and astronomical wonders and people growing faint: the main thing is that there will be Jesus. "Then they will see the Son of Man coming in a cloud with power and great glory. Now when these things begin to take place, stand up and raise your heads, because your redemption is drawing near."

Now who knows whether when things come to an end—old movements, old relationships, our lives, our history—who knows whether when things come to an end the Jesus who meets us there will be sitting on clouds of glory with trumpets sounding. Maybe first Advent and second Advent do come together, and Christ has a way of sneaking up on us every time. In seeming ordinary places and inconspicuous ways. Truth is, I think it's a better bet to look around you for Jesus than to check the clouds, but who knows for sure?

What we do know for sure is the promise: all kinds of things end. Heaven and earth will pass away. But Christ does not end. God's reaching out to us in Christ does not end.

So, in the midst of endings and losses and uncertainties we live with—hope!

A woman I knew and loved named Marion Kenyon had more than her share of losses. A child lost just after childbirth. A husband lost first to crippling illness and then after seventeen years of convalescence to death. She suffered the loss of her own health, slowly, steadily. At her memorial service her minister read a poem she had given him long years before.

> If but one message I may leave behind,
> One single word of comfort for my kind,
> It would be this,
> O brother, sister, friend,
> Whatever life may bring or God may send,
> Take heart and wait.
>
> Despair may tangle darkly at your feet
> And hope once cool and sweet
> Be lost. But suddenly above a hill

A heavenly lamp set on a heavenly sill
Will shine for you
And point the way to go.

How well I know
For I have waited through the dark,
And I have seen a star rise in the blackest sky, repeatedly.
It has not failed me yet,
And I have learned
God never will forget
To light his lamp
If we but wait for it,
It will be lit.

In light of these last things, we wait in hope.

IV

And this, too. In the light of last things, we concentrate on first things. Matters of first importance. If it is true that all things pass away but that all things pass away toward God in Jesus Christ, then we hold fast to what matters most. In Luke Jesus says it this way: "Be on guard so that your hearts are not weighed down with dissipation and drunkenness and the worries of this life. Stand up! Lift up your heads. Your redemption is drawing nigh."

If time keeps moving and histories and programs and relationships and lives keep ending, what do we hold onto? First things. The things that matter. God's love, the people God has given us, integrity, compassion, some vision larger than our own bank accounts, some hope more encompassing than a better car and early retirement.

A man I knew and loved named Glenn Brown discovered when he was thirty-five years old that he had inoperable cancer. He kept a journal of his last days, full of doubt and faith and sorrow and surprising joy. Most of all full of the firm determination to hold onto what mattered most: first things for the last days.

What mattered most was God: "At least I know the precious value of what remains," wrote Glenn, "and I am blessed with having time to face the end . . . I know life is a gift and I have no claim except to that which is given. My strength and courage are from beyond me, from God."

What mattered most were the people he loved: "In dying I know what I already knew in life and couldn't live with, that it is the other people I love who matter most."

What mattered most was the world in which he lived, which lived in him: "When we finally realize that life is really sacred, we feel a kinship with birds and trees and growing things. You see in other life something that is in your life, and you respect that life and all life (as God's gift)."

Meanwhile of course (he wrote about this, too), while he held fast to what mattered most, Glenn mowed the lawn and dried the dishes and paid the bills and went to parent-teacher conferences. But he held his head high; waited for his redemption.

When Glenn Brown's journals were published, the book was called *Life is a Gift*. That's what his living and his dying showed. Life is a gift; Christ is a gift.

At Bethlehem and every day and at the end of days. From Christ life comes, to Christ life returns.

We hope, we hold fast, we wait.

Happy Advent.

Amen.

June 25, 1995 ·
Battell Chapel ·
1 Kings 19:1-18, Luke 8

*William Sloane Coffin, whom Dean Bartlett mentions in
the following sermon, was Chaplain of Yale University for
many years, and—particularly in the 1960s—was a
powerful voice against racial segregation and American
military involvement in Viet Nam.*

I

Martin Luther King, tired and discouraged, tired of fighting
for justice and discouraged at the lack of progress, has just settled
in to bed when the phone rings: "Listen, nigger, we've taken all
we want from you. Before next week you'll be sorry you ever
came to Montgomery." Then King says he got up, went to the
kitchen, and complained to God: "I am here taking a stand for
what I believe is right. But now I am afraid. The people are looking
to me for leadership, and if I stand before them without strength
and courage, they too will falter. I am at the end of my powers. I
have nothing left."

The prophet Elijah, tired and discouraged, tired of fighting
for God against Ahab and Jezebel and the priests of Baal,
discouraged at the lack of progress: "It is enough O Lord, now
take away my life, for I am no better than my ancestors."

"What are you doing, Elijah?" asks the Lord. Elijah answers:
"I have been very zealous for the Lord, the God of hosts; for the

Israelites have forsaken your covenant, thrown down your altars, and killed your prophets with the sword. I alone am left, and they are seeking my life, to take it away."

Discouraged heroes; exhausted prophets. Teetering between disappointment and self-pity. We don't pretend to reach their heroism but we do understand the disappointments.

We, too, have given huge chunks of our lives to causes that seem to be faltering.

We have loved social justice and believed in the obligation of government of the people and by the people to be FOR the people, too. We have hoped for congruity between individual ethics and social responsibility: if we are asked to be compassionate, one by one, why can't we build compassionate communities?

But the problems seem to grow faster than the solutions. Poverty is a strong enemy, not easily thwarted. A drug culture multiplies crimes and cripples our cities. Political selflessness comes under suspicion. We are told that there is nothing we can do as the body politic. Each of us for herself. Disappointing, discouraging.

"We have been very zealous for the Lord, the God of hosts, but people have forsaken your covenant, thrown down your altars and ignored your prophets. Truth is I'm about the only one left, and I'm weakening."

We have loved the church, maybe even loved this church. Certainly loved churches like this that try to hold together the life of the Spirit and the life of the world. We have loved churches that tried to hold together mind and soul. Love the Lord with all our heart and with all our minds; not be afraid to ask tough questions. Skeptical of authority and scared of authoritarians. Those are the churches we love.

But it seems to be a losing battle. We're caught between the absolutely certain on the one side and the unashamedly secular on the other. The mainline churches are the old line churches, outfoxed by Fundamentalists and ignored by the culture. The Church of Christ in Yale seems like an anachronism: who besides us cares? And there aren't many of us left.

"We have been very zealous for the Lord, the God of hosts, yet culture and University have forsaken the covenant, ignored the altar and turned a deaf ear to more recent chaplains. There are only a very few of us left."

We sympathize with Elijah and we sympathize with King. Even for us second rank faithful folk it's hard to see your zeal ignored and your faith derided. We begin to feel not only lonely but sorry for ourselves. We're all there is. We only are left.

II

Of course you heard the story of Elijah as we read it a few minutes ago. As usual in biblical stories God gets the last word, and the last word doesn't leave much room for self-pity. In fact the last word doesn't leave much room for SELF.

As is so typical with God, when God gets to talking, God wants to talk about God. As is so typical with God, when God talks about God, we find that our lives begin to tilt toward hope.

Here's what God says about God to Elijah (and to King) and then to us.

First thing God says: God is often softer than we think.

A great deal of scholarly ink is spilt over the episode of the wind, earthquake, fire and the still small voice, which the NRSV (perhaps influenced by Simon and Garfunkel) now translates: "the sound of sheer silence"—

It may be all right that no one knows exactly what the phrase means. We do know what it demonstrates. That sometimes God isn't there in the big, extraordinary, headline grabbing moments— the earthquake, wind and fire. Sometimes God is there in something smaller, softer, and enduring.

Maybe the cause of social justice in our time is served not by sensational legislation but by the fidelity of those who won't give in to the currents of sanctified selfishness.

Those who hold fast, do what there is to do, dwell in our cities, act civilly, vote faithfully, join the PTA, break down barriers, hold out hands. The quiet people blessed by the quiet God.

When King got so discouraged all the noise was on the other side. The rude loudness of the phone that roused him in the night. The shouts of people who hated him. The noise of politicians for the most part pontificating about states' rights.

He might have hoped for God to be as loud as the earthquake, wind and fire. The voice he got was small, internal, quiet: strong. "At the moment of my distress," said King, "it seemed as though I could hear the quiet assurance of an inner voice, saying: 'Stand up for righteousness. Stand up for truth. God will be at your side forever.' Almost at once my fears began to pass from me . . . the outer situation remained the same but God had given me inner calm."

After the wind the earthquake, and after the earthquake the fire. And God was not in earthquake, wind or fire. But after that: the sound of sheer, redemptive silence.

I spent most of the week at the national meetings of the American Baptists, my denomination. Like so many other mainline denominations we're facing the possibility of splitting, and again as with many other denominations what may split us is the debate over how to interpret the Bible when it comes to having churches that welcome gay and Lesbian people.

There's a lot of noise saying that we have to close doors and close ranks. Some executive ministers—powerful leaders of our various regions—are talking very loudly about disfellowshipping churches that are open and affirming. Our denomination may be rent by a kind of theological earthquake: it's not clear whether the center can hold.

One night in the midst of Baptist earthquake, wind and fire a smaller group of Baptists gathered away from the crowd in a friendly UCC Church. One Baptist minister who's a hospital chaplain has come out as a gay man, and the question is whether the denomination will take away his chaplaincy credentials. He was the speaker for this event.

The program began with a very soft voice. The chaplain's father got up to introduce his son. The chaplain's father is an executive minister. One of the few quiet ones among the fairly noisy executives arguing back and forth.

"I want to introduce my son," he said. "He is a Christian, a Baptist and an ordained minister. He is also a gay man who lives with his partner. His mother and I are so proud of him."

The big noises may not be very encouraging. But God still whispers hope and truth. After earthquake, wind and fire, the still small voice.

III

So God speaks to the discouraged prophet. God is softer than we sometimes think. No less real, just a lot more quiet.

And this, too: God is stronger than we sometimes think. Self-pity, even prophetic self-pity, tends to forget how much more is going on. "I alone am left," says Elijah.

"Oh, come on," says the Lord God. "I can vouch for seven thousand whose knees have not bowed to Baal, seven thousand whose mouths have not kissed that false god."

Listen, we worry about the failure of the social causes to which we have given our time and energy. Sometimes our causes will fail, sometimes they will succeed. But, the failure of our cause is not the failure of God. God is stronger and sneakier than the best of our causes, and here and there throughout this land and throughout the whole creation, knees refuse to bow and lips confessing Jesus Christ is Lord will not kiss the idols of selfishness and greed and power. Keep your eyes open! Keep your ears open! Lift your hearts.

We worry about denominations and congregations that don't have the power we once did. And we're right about that. I saw in the *New Haven Register* a couple of weeks ago someone's list of the ten most important things that had happened in his decades in New Haven and number six was a sermon Bill Coffin preached standing right here. But that was more than twenty years ago, and I doubt that any sermon preached anywhere in a mainline church in this town will make anybody's top ten important events for as long as we all shall live.

But that doesn't mean it doesn't count. It doesn't mean that the witness of those who believe in faith and action, piety and thoughtfulness doesn't matter. We may not be millions, but there are seven thousand of us, and that counts, spreads, endures.

I went last week to the funeral service for Gin Wu. Gin Wu was 101 years old. He came to this country about 1910 from China and he felt pretty much isolated and left out, especially ignored by the European Americans who got here before him.

Except for Calvary Baptist Church. Calvary Baptist Church in downtown New Haven had a church school class for Chinese people, and they welcomed Gin Wu. So he stayed in New Haven and endured.

He and his wife had children, and all the children went to college, and then grandchildren, and then great grandchildren. They were all there for the service. Engineers, public school teachers, physicians, lawyers, the head of Sara Lee Food's Asian offices, and presiding—one grandson who is a Baptist minister. Maybe Gin Wu would have made it in America and all those impressive people eighty-five years later would be strengthening the forces of generosity in our society. But maybe not. Maybe it took Calvary Baptist Church reaching out to Chinese people to make it work. Anyway, today all those Wus around the world honor their grandfather who honored the church that touched him. But the church is no longer there. It closed in May of 1994. An easy time for sorrow and self-pity. But the wrong time, too. That church is gone, but seventy—who knows, seven thousand folk don't bow to Baal or kiss the idols . . . they remain. God is stronger than we think.

IV

And God is tougher than we like. The lectionary committee, those who suggest our weekly Scripture verses, left out the punch line from this tale of Elijah: they give us the sweetness of God but not the sternness. After all the comfort God goes on. "Listen," God says to the prophet: "Stop being discouraged, or more accurately, stop feeling sorry for yourself. Go, return on your way to the wilderness of Damascus, when you arrive you shall anoint Hazael as King over Aram, and you shall anoint Jehu as king over Israel, and you shall anoint Elisha as prophet to succeed you."

Thanks very much, Elijah. I have enjoyed this little therapeutic hour together. But I am still God and you are still my prophet. Get to work.

Jesus, in the story from Luke, cures a man who's been driven mad by demons. So of course the man is deeply grateful and just wants to cling to Jesus forever. Keep that religious high going. But listen to Luke's Gospel: "Jesus sent him away, saying, "Return to your home and declare how much God has done for you."

All right, Elijah, now you've had time to feel bad about yourself. All right recovering demoniac, you've had time to feel good about yourself. Enough, there's work to be done. Get to work.

I'd read the Martin Luther King sermon about his great discouragement maybe a dozen times, caught God's softness and caught God's strength but only this week preparing this sermon caught God's toughness, too: I remembered that the still small voice said to King: "I will be at your side forever." I forgot what else the still small voice said: "Get up, Martin. On your feet. Stand up for righteousness. Stand up for truth."

I forgot what King said about God's promise: "That word will give our tired feet new strength as we continue our forward stride toward the city of freedom. Our God is able to make a way out of no way, and to transform dark yesterdays into bright tomorrows."

Listen, beloved, I know that our cities aren't what we'd hoped and our nation isn't what we'd hoped and our churches certainly aren't what we had hoped.

It's tough.

Only God is tougher.

Go on Elijah, back to the wilderness of Damascus. Anoint
me two kings and one prophet.

I am still God and there is still work to be done.

Go, Elijah, go.

Amen.

September 22, 1995 ·
Yale Divinity School ·
Luke 15:1-10

Every Friday at Yale Divinity School, the Eucharist is celebrated in Marquand Chapel at the regular Chapel time, as opposed to the other days of the week when worship does not include Eucharist. This sermon was preached at a Friday Eucharist Chapel service.

I

Fridays in Marquand are hard on us Baptists. First of all, the Lord's Supper, which we know and love to celebrate—about once a month—gets dubbed "the Eucharist." Second, the trays with little cups full of Welch's Grape Juice that our Lord served to the disciples are replaced with chalices of wine. And, hardest of all for the preacher, the freedom of the Spirit gives way to the lectionary.

The truth is, I thought I'd lucked out this year, because I was told that the assigned Gospel reading for today was Luke 15. "Terrific," I thought. I've got about twelve sermons on Luke 15, eight on the prodigal son and four on the older brother. I'd preached at least six of the prodigal son sermons before the Chair of the Trustees Board stopped me after church. "I'm tired of hearing about that younger brother," he said. "I've tried to do what's right all my life. I identify much more with the older brother."

I soon discovered that about half the people in the congregation identify more with the older brother, so I added to my sermons a variety of homilies on the theme of staying at home and sometimes feeling aggrieved about not getting your due.

Identifying, of course, is the clue to the story of the Prodigal Son and/or the Older Brother. We love to hear the story and sermons on the story because we all identify with one sibling or the other—or both. And those of us who have learned to enjoy narrative preaching love to preach on the parable because it's the closest thing to a full blown short story we've got in the New Testament, and because we get to ask the key question for any good narrative sermon: "With whom do we want the congregation to identify this week?"

II

But who can identify with the lost sheep or the missing coin? (The bad news, as you've just heard, is that this is what the lectionary assigns me, not the brothers with whom we can empathize so readily.) We haven't a clue to the internal life of a lamb or a drachma, either one. Does the sheep, having wandered far from the fold, come to itself and repent of its prodigality? Does the coin, in its isolated corner, notice that the other nine are having so much fun in the purse and regret its fake self-sufficiency? Of course not.

Our text this morning gives us no surrogate selves to help us with our issues of identity. We know nothing of the implicit or explicit faith of the sheep, nor of the penitence of the coin. They are not the subjects of the text, nor the objects of our gaze. Luke in fact tells us what the issue is: "The Pharisees and the scribes were grumbling and saying, 'This fellow welcomes sinners and eats with them.'"

For now "this fellow" is the one we think about. The host at the table, not the guests. For now the issue is not sinners, sheep, or coin—or us. For now the issue is: Who is this fellow? What does God do in him?

III

This fellow who eats with sinners is like a shepherd, leaving ninety and nine behind to seek out one. In the church of my childhood there hung a picture of the shepherd reaching out for the sheep. Somewhat hazy and haloed to be sure, a little romantic for my later taste, but what sticks in my mind is the fact that the shepherd was leaning precariously over the cliff to reach the sheep. As if, in seeking, the shepherd left not just the ninety-nine but his own safety behind—a quest almost foolhardy in its riskiness.

This fellow who eats with sinners is like a woman with ten silver coins, who loses one and turns the house upside down until she finds it. Maybe that's just prudence. If you've only got a dollar, every dime counts. But as you look at the story, what starts out looking frugal ends up looking nearly spendthrift. The woman lights every light. She sweeps and scrubs and scours and searches. All that oil burnt, all that energy spent. A single minded longing for the lost.

"Who is this fellow who eats with sinners?" our text asks. Not who are we, but who is he? Not what is it like to be a prodigal or an elder brother or a lost sheep or a missing coin, but who is the one who chases after sheep, crawls around looking for coins, heads out seeking for daughters and sons?

IV

Beloved, this early in the semester and in our careers and in our lives, before we have had time to worry any more about our salvation or our vocation, and certainly before we begin worrying about our transcript, the Gospel invites us to think on the one who saves us and the one who calls us. The Gospel invites us to praise the one who alone in heaven or on earth deserves the highest honors God can give.

Even as we come to his table, before we have much time for self-examination or self-doubt, we are invited to turn our gaze upon Jesus, our host—in Eucharist—in thanksgiving.

For before you knew how to seek for anything, God in Christ was seeking you—like a foolhardy shepherd risking life and limb to reach a sheep, like a woman one coin short who diligently, passionately, won't give up until the lost is found.

Like an old father sitting on a porch who sees his child heading down the road, and not counting his dignity a thing to be hoarded, empties himself, hitches up his skirts or hitches up his trousers, scrambles down the steps and scurries down the road—to throw his arms around you, and to bring you home.

To Christ be thanks and praise.

October 8, 1995 ·
Battell Chapel ·
Habakkuk 1:1-4, 2:1-4,
Luke 17:1-10

*The court case Dean Bartlett mentions in this sermon is
the O.J. Simpson murder trial, which ended just days before
this sermon was preached with the jury acquitting Simpson
of the murders.*

I

In the church of my youth in Los Angeles, one of the pillars
of faith was a woman named Mrs. Bibby. In addition to having a
firm belief in what she considered the literal meaning of every
verse of Scripture, Mrs. Bibby had an unshakeable belief in the
power of prayer. Even in those days Los Angeles was a crowded
city, long on cars and short on parking. Nothing daunted, Mrs.
Bibby was famous for driving directly where she wanted to go
and praying for a parking place. Miraculously, time after time, a
Buick or a Packard eased out of a comfortably large space just in
front of her, traffic parted and Mrs. Bibby pulled in.

At first glance it looks as though Jesus words to the apostles
in Luke's Gospel were made just for the Mrs. Bibbys of this world.
If you have a mustard seed of faith you can say to the mulberry
tree that blocks your ocean view, jump up and be planted in the

sea, and the tree will obey. Say to the Buick move and it will move, to the Packard, out of my way and behold, a parking place. However, the context of the apostles' odd request makes it clear that something more is at stake here than displaced trees or easy parking. Jesus has just warned the disciples about the difficulty of the faithful life. If you cause other folk to go astray, you might better have a millstone tied around your neck and be cast into the sea along with the transplanted mulberry tree. If someone sins against you seven times in the same day, and seven times repents—seven times you must forgive.

It's hard to spend your life trying to keep from tripping up other people; it's even harder to forgive and forgive and forgive. It's tough business to live a life where people care for other people and where the most important business of every day is the business of reconciliation.

No wonder the disciples listen to the difficult demands of the Gospel and say: "Lord, increase our faith!" They've got it halfway right. On our own it's as hard for people like us to care for the least among us and to forgive and forgive and forgive, it's as hard for us to do that as for a mulberry tree to uproot itself from the bank and grow afresh in the bottom of the sea. Left to ourselves we're not great at caring and we're not great at reconciling.

"Lord, increase our faith!"

II

Now Jesus' reply seems straightforward enough: "If you have faith the size of a mustard seed, you could say to this mulberry tree, be uprooted and planted in the sea, and it would obey you." But, at least as Luke tells the story, our Lord's syntax is a little confusing.

Maybe he's saying: "You poor disciples, you haven't got what it takes. If only you had a mustard seed's worth of faith you could accomplish miracles."

But maybe he's saying: "Don't worry so much about it. Since

you've already have a mustard seed's worth of faith, you can accomplish miracles."

I've got to tell you I like the second version better. The actual words of the sentence won't tell you for sure it's the right version, but I notice that Luke has been calling the disciples disciples and now he calls them apostles. Apostle is a term of great honor for Luke. This reminds the readers that these people DID accomplish miracles, healed people, preached the Gospel, founded churches—far more astonishing than the simple feat of trees jumping into the sea.

So give me the benefit of the doubt. Let's hear the text my way: "Lord," they say (and we say) "increase our faith." And Jesus says: "Since you've already got a mustard seed's worth of faith, you can take on the difficult tasks of discipleship. You can care for those who need your care and you can forgive those who do you wrong. You can work reconciliation."

But why would Jesus say the apostles have a mustard seed's worth of faith? Because they ask for more faith. Here is good news for today. Asking for faith is the beginning of faith. Wanting to trust is the beginning of trust. Seeking for God is the beginning of finding. Maybe not all we want, but for today, all we need. A mustard seed.

III

Dorothy Day is one of my heroes. She early developed a passion for caring for those in need and for working reconciliation among people. For a long time she hoped that Marxist ideology and strenuous work would give her all she needed to serve the community for which she longed.

But it also happened that as she sought a better society, she gave birth to a daughter, Tamara. As Dorothy thought about Tamara's future: "I knew that I was going to have my child baptized," Dorothy later wrote, "cost what it may. I knew that I was not going to have her floundering through many years as I had done, doubting and hesitating and undisciplined. I felt it was the greatest thing I could do for my child. For myself I prayed the gift of faith. I was sure, yet not sure."

For myself I prayed the gift of faith. Asking for faith is the beginning of faith. The mustard seed. Tamara was baptized, and then, almost to keep her company, Dorothy was baptized, too.

At first the worship, the sacraments, the catechism were only obligations, till through prayer and practice and patience they became not obligations but joy.

And then through reading and study and friendships, Dorothy found a way to inspire her love of community and her dream of reconciliation. With others she founded the Catholic Worker movement where for decades now faithful people have done what Jesus told the apostles to do: care for those who struggle, reconcile those who need reconciliation.

Dorothy Day called the first part of her life "The Long Loneliness," and it was a long way home from loneliness, too. But the first step was there in the love for her daughter, and the second step in getting Tamara baptized, and then her own baptism and on and on, farther and deeper surely than she dreamed she would ever go.

Asking for faith is the beginning of faith.

"Lord increase our faith," say the apostles.

"Start with what you've got." he says. "For now, a mustard seed will do."

IV

The apostles beg Jesus for faith. The prophet Habakkuk begs God for justice. "O Lord, how long shall I cry for help, and you will not listen? Or cry to you, 'violence,' and you will not save? Why do you make me see wrongdoing and look at trouble? The law becomes slack, and justice never prevails."

Hard times in Judah. Pressure from without, terrible divisions among the people. Cries for justice that apparently go unheeded.

What these last few days have made us think about is not so much the complications of the judicial system or the ambiguities of one particular case. What we've had to think about is how divided our nation still can be. How differently people of goodwill experience what it is to be American.

Recalling Mrs. Bibby driving around the streets of Los Angeles, I recalled Stan Sanders, too. Stan and I were both active in student government in L.A. in the fifties, he at one high school and I at another. But there were conferences for budding politicians, and we got to know each other fairly well, visited each other's homes, went to church together once or twice. I would have said that life was treating us both fairly well. That L.A. was a good place for both of us to grow up.

Then we went our separate ways to college; in the terrible wake of deprivation and injustice riots broke out in Watts. Anger, destruction, distress. I picked up *Life* magazine to see the pictures, and there, the opening article, was an interview with Stan Sanders. I had never dreamed what it felt like to him, growing up in the city we shared. Powers that seemed to me benign had proved oppressive. Issues I missed hit him every day. I thought we were pretty good friends, and I didn't even know the neighborhood he lived in was called Watts.

Like any number of other Los Angeles young people, I oozed goodwill and missed the point. There are divides that are very hard to bridge and histories that separate more than they unite. Justice is slack, not just this week or that week, but week after week after week. Habakkuk had it about right: "O Lord, how long shall I cry for help and you will not listen?"

V

But then of course the Lord does listen, does respond. "There is still a vision for the appointed time. If it seems to tarry, wait for it. It will surely come, it will not delay. Look at the proud! their spirit is not right in them. But the righteous live by their faith."

"Look at the proud! their spirit is not right in them." We have been proud enough. Proud of our comfort, our accomplishments, our security. Proud of our tolerance. Sure that with just a little goodwill we can undo centuries of injustice. Just invite Stan Sanders to a party, and by God! we have overcome.

But the righteous live by faith. By the hope that God works every day to break down barriers, to broaden perspectives, to punish oppression, and to work righteousness.

What God's vision demands of us is the most difficult combination of patience and action. To stand strong like Habakkuk at our watch post, but to stand in hope and faith because, God help us, we need God's help.

Jesus tells the disciples: asking for faith is the beginning of faith.

God tells Habakkuk: hoping for justice is the beginning of justice.

Keep hoping, keep working. The righteous will live by faith.

VI

Another California city, Oakland, at about the same time Stan Sanders and I were growing up in Los Angeles. African Americans had returned to Oakland or moved to Oakland after the war, and because of the GI Bill they been able to afford good educations, and the economy was doing well, and some of them had after all fought for their country. So a number began to move from the flatlands, which had been Oakland's ghetto, to the hills above the lake, where the white folk lived.

For Sale signs started going up all over the neighborhood. So the pastor of the neighborhood church and the principal of the neighborhood school went calling, every night. When they called on new neighbors, they welcomed them to the neighborhood and invited them to visit the church and to visit the school. When they called on old neighbors they encouraged them to stay and to join the welcome, too.

It wasn't a perfect solution, far from it. But forty years later the neighborhood is still the most integrated neighborhood in the most integrated city in America, and the church's membership is about forty seven percent black and forty seven per cent white and six percent Asian American and Hispanic.

Because a couple of people hoped and worked. Righteous people, who lived by faith.

VII

Asking for faith is the beginning of faith.
Hoping for justice is the beginning of justice.
Start with a mustard seed, and see what God will do.
One of the old rabbis told this story about the crossing of the Red Sea. God had promised Moses that God would part the sea so that the Israelites could escape from Pharaoh. But when the children of Israel got to the shore, the Egyptian chariots chasing close behind them, there was the sea, deep, wet, wavy and unmoved.

Until by faith, the first Israelite took the first step into the sea—then the waters parted and God's people walked toward freedom.

One step. Like a mustard seed. Like a prayer for faith. Like a hope for justice.

Keep hoping.
Keep working.
The righteous live by faith.
Amen.
May it be so for us. Amen.

May 27, 1996 ·
Yale Divinity School ·
Acts 2:1-14, 1
Corinthians 12:1-13

The following sermon was offered at the Commencement Eucharist service for the graduating class of 1996.

I

During his last year of seminary, when he should have been writing papers or practicing sermons, Martin Marty the church historian, along with several of his classmates, invented a fictional theologian: Franz Bibfeldt. At a time when dialectical theology reigned supreme and the leading thinkers of the church were passionately taking sides against the world and sometimes against each other, the fictional Bibfeldt tried to find a middle way. His dissertation was entitled: "The Paradox Relieved." And all his fictional writings tried either to get the reader off the horns of a dilemma or to deny that there really was a dilemma at all.

Bibfeldt lives to this day among Marty's students and friends. Two alleged Bibfeldtian tomes remain firmly in my memory, or imagination.

One was the pamphlet Bibfeldt wrote just after Karl Barth had thundered his response to what he saw as the capitulation to natural theology in the work of his former friend. Barth's paper, you'll remember was entitled simply, "Nein, Emil Brunner." A few days later Bibfeldt sent Brunner his own reflection entitled, "Well, Maybe."

The other vintage Bibfeldtian publication was his lengthy reflection on Kierkegaard's masterpiece, "Either/Or." Bibfeldt entitled his response: "Both/And."

It struck me in re-reading the Pentecost passage in the Book of Acts that St. Luke and Franz Bibfeldt have something in common. While Luke is much clearer on his convictions than Bibfeldt is, nonetheless, Luke and Acts are perhaps the center of Both/And theology in the New Testament.

Not the church for Jews or the church for Gentiles, but the church for Jews and Gentiles. Not the apostle Paul vs. the apostle Peter (as we find them in Galatians), but Paul and Peter, joined together in the spreading of the Gospel.

We have had plenty of crises in your years here, and there will probably be more to come, but the truth is that like St. Luke, we, too, are probably in it for the long haul: the words of Acts may provide a vision worthy of our considering. Not always Either/Or. Sometimes Both/And.

II

Take the Pentecost story. It is obviously and blessedly a story of inclusiveness. As our liturgy this morning reminds us, Pentecost is a Babel-reverser; turns the story of confounded language right around. All those people sent from the city into the corners of the world with tongues confounded now return to the city to Jerusalem and behold! they understand one another's speech.

But the Babel-reverser doesn't exactly reverse Babel, after all. Before Babel, the whole earth had one language and the same words. At Pentecost, though all the people do now understand one another's speech, they do not all speak one language. After Pentecost there is still the whole multitude of languages—Parthian and Mede and Phrygian and Coptic and

Latin and Arabic—but despite the languages and through the languages—behold! those who are filled with God's Spirit now do understand each other's speech.

You know the old paradox of the happy fall. Had our first ancestors not sinned we would not have needed to be redeemed, and yet the gifts of Golgotha are richer than the fruits of Eden any day. Maybe there is another paradox here, that the fall from Babel was a happy fall as well, because a church speaking a multitude of languages but united in the Spirit is a richer community than the old mono-linguistic gang that built the tower all those years ago. The diverse gifts of Pentecost are richer far than the uniformity Babel's tower destroyed.

To hear some people talk you'd think the only hope for the church was to find a kind of theological Esperanto, a universal tongue—the one language and the one vocabulary that we all could share. The language God thinks in if you will. I doubt if we can find that language; I'm not sure we want that language. Hebrews says "In many and diverse ways God spoke to us by the prophets, but in these last days God has spoken to us by a Son."

Pentecost suggests that we can also speak of the Son in many and diverse ways. We need at least a thousand tongues to sing our great redeemer's praise.

But! And here's the Both/And. But it is for our redeemer's praise that we need the tongues to sing. The miracle is not that all these people can hear the apostles speaking in their diverse tongues—Luke says the miracle is that in their diverse tongues all these people hear the apostles speaking "about God's deeds of power."

At Pentecost the celebration leads to a sermon and the sermon leads to the heart of the matter. Here is the punch line of Peter's sermon. "Listen to what I have to say, Jesus of Nazareth, a man attested to you by God with deeds of power, wonders and signs that God did through him among you—this man you crucified and killed, but God has raised him up, having freed him from death."

On the one hand the diversity of our tongues. On the other hand the centrality of the Gospel. Oh for a thousand tongues to sing our great redeemer's praise.

To hear some people talk you'd think that we are given the diversity of languages mostly in order to praise the diversity of languages. Then at Pentecost the Cretans should have declared how proud they were to be Cretans, and the Pamphylians chatted about the Pamphylian experience and the Egyptians testified about how special it is to speak in Coptic. But the Gospel all these people hear is not first of all about themselves: it is first of all about the God who made them in all their diversity, and redeems them, in all their diversity, and speaks to them in a thousand tongues—but speaks of the ONE who is redeemer, Christ Jesus crucified and risen once again.

Or as the non-Bibfeldtian St. Paul puts it: "as the body, though many, is one body, so it is with Christ . . . and we are all made to drink of one Spirit." Both the many-ness and the oneness are the gift.

III

Another Both/And, too. When Peter explains Pentecost to the astonished onlookers, he turns where Christian witnesses always turn—to Scripture. The sermon with which Christian church begins turns to Hebrew Scripture, Old Testament, it begins with Joel—and runs through parts of three psalms, two prophets and at least two references to the deuteronomic history before Peter is through. At its center is what became the center of the New Testament, the apostolic testimony to Christ crucified and risen again.

If you have learned one thing at this place, from our obsessive insistence that you get immersed in Scripture—if you have learned one thing here it is that Scripture shapes lives and churches and the way we see history and the way we intend the world. Thirty three years ago I arrived as a student full of philosophical questions and annoyed that Davie Napier, our Old

Testament professor, insisted that we actually take a test on the content of the Old Testament. I didn't give up on the questions, but Scripture took hold in a way I would scarcely have dreamed. Like God's own love it will not let you go.

But do notice, too, that Peter's sermon isn't about Scripture only. There is also this event to interpret, this astonishing, multi-faceted, multi-lingual, spirit filled, spirit inebriated celebration that must be explained.

Christian witness takes place at the intersection of Scripture and event. The bravest and most essential Christian witness doesn't say just what God does in the Bible but in the light of Scripture what God does in the world.

Here Both/And transcends Either/Or. If Luke is right the Either Scripture/Or experience division may not be as helpful as we'd thought. There is no way to read Scripture without attending to our experience, because WE are the ones who read it. There is no way to read experience without attending to Scripture because we are Christian people and the Bible is the light God sheds upon our sometimes darkening world.

A few years ago I was teaching a course on preaching social issues, and one student in the class was Mary Ogumba who was spending one year as a special student from Ghana. Mary's text was the song of that other Mary, when the angel tells her she will bear a child:

"My soul doth magnify the Lord."

"I know how she felt," said Mary Ogumba. "For here I was, a poor person where only the wealthy had power, a woman where only the men had authority, and through my church God said to me, "Mary, we will make you a minister of the Gospel. We will give you money to go to America and study. You will return and serve your people."

"Oh," said Mary Ogumba. "My soul doth magnify the Lord!"

Was that Scripture shedding light on experience or experience shedding light on Scripture? It was both of course, with no room to drive the thinnest wedge between them.

St. Peter combining Scripture and the astonishing tongues to make a sermon. St. Paul combining Scripture and the stumbling attempts of the Corinthians to be community to make a letter. We turn to Scripture and discover that Scripture does not confine its wisdom to itself; it sheds light also on the world—God's world.

IV

What Franz Bibfeldt does jokingly St. Luke does with absolute seriousness—tries to hold together what we are too eager to tear asunder. The diversity of our many tongues but the centrality of our one Christ; the power of Scripture to illumine the world and the power of the world to open us to Scripture.

I needed to find a picture or two to drive it home, and I found two.

You are one picture, YDS class of 1996. Diverse in many ways. Talking in such different tongues: Eucharist or Lord's Supper, service or mass, sanctuary or auditorium, catechesis or Christian education. Heading for such different vocations— pastorates, priesthoods, teaching, libraries, social work. Bringing such different histories and loyalties and affections and passions. And yet such astonishing unity. You have been drawn together around a Chapel, which even when we only feel guilty for skipping, is center of our lives as Christ is center of the diverse church. You have been drawn together to argue—which is its own form of witnessing, its own Pentecost, caring enough about each other to listen, caring enough about the truth to believe that the argument has a point and a purpose and a goal.

You are a picture of the blessed tension between your story and the biblical story. Forgive me if I speak here of the way I know you best; through the sermons I have heard many of you preach. Two things happen in that preaching. The Bible begins to shape your experience. We hear you deepen and strengthen and tradition yourselves. Your experience shapes the way we hear the Bible. The best part of my job is letting you show me what is really there in Scripture, but I hadn't seen before, because I didn't have your eyes. Both/And.

One other picture. This communion table shows forth what our passage speaks. Diversity and unity are joined here. This is a table open to the most astonishing diversity of Christ's people. As we serve communion here we do not check doctrine or ethnic background or ask who you're in love with or how you voted.

But it isn't just an open table, either. It is Christ's table. When we come here, with whatever mix of hopes and fears and doubts and faith we discover what the church has always known. That he is here. And that the most important gift of our diversity is that God has provided diverse ways of thanking Christ our Lord.

This table shows forth what our passage speaks. Scripture marries with event. When Jesus called the first apostles to this table, he turned to Scripture to make clear the meaning of this meal. Passover, covenant, sacrifice—the old and blessed words that shed light on that night and on the day that was to come.

But what Jesus Christ made clear was also something bold, astonishing and new—not God in the book only, but God present in the bread and in the wine, and then tomorrow, Friday, God present on the cross, and then on Sunday—God triumphant—not just in the book, but in the world.

> Dearly beloved,
> come to the table,
> cherish the book,
> serve God,
> love God's world.
> Amen.

September 6, 1996 ·
Yale Divinity School ·
Luke 10:38-42,
1 Corinthians 14:13-19

The new Dean of the Divinity School mentioned in this sermon is Richard Wood, Dean of Yale Divinity School from 1996-2000. Guy Martin, also mentioned, was the Dean of Admissions of the Divinity School for many years.

I

As usual there is trouble in Corinth. The congregation is divided in more ways than scholars have ever been able to figure out, but one division is clear enough. Some of the Corinthian Christians are long on enthusiasm and short on logic, and others are long on wisdom and short on joy. Paul envisions a church where wisdom is tempered by delight and where excitement can still speak in coherent sentences.

In the first part of the letter Paul is reminding those enamored of logic and eloquence that in Jesus Christ we know a blessed foolishness not even the most careful formula can catch. In the last part of the letter Paul is reminding those whose capacity for enthusiasm has outdistanced their capacity for clarity that divine foolishness should not be confused with human gibberish.

In the passage we read this morning, the issue is how the Corinthians are to worship, and Paul brings his two concerns together. "I will pray with the spirit, but I will pray with the mind also; I will sing praise with the spirit, but I will sing praise with the mind also."

A few years ago the University of Chicago alumni magazine had a reflection piece by a young woman who sings in the Rockefeller Chapel Choir. She writes of how when she got to the University the pressures of studying hard and thinking well so overwhelmed her that she had a hard time justifying sneaking off for choir practice or Sunday worship. But in time the Chapel became not obligation but gift, and it was gift in part because it didn't just provide something to think about. It provided something to sing about.

"For one morning and one evening a week," she writes. "I can think in different ways and about different things than I do with my work. Singing is communication through words of course, but also through emotions and beauty. You can't be worried about your scholarship when you're worrying about whether you're breathing properly."

Breathing properly, living properly, isn't only a matter of thinking. It's also a matter of knowing when to make beauty, or honor beauty, or worship the God of beauty.

What some Corinthians are leaving out of their lives are prayer and music. They search up and down for the meaning of creation but never sit still to worship the creator. They have lots of facts, but the facts don't turn out to point to anything beside themselves. They have encyclopedic minds, but their lives are encyclopedic too: one thing after another without focus, purpose, plot, delight or hope.

When we talk about this Divinity School we say that worship is central to our life as Marquand Chapel is central to the Quad. Our new Dean hasn't been here long enough to distinguish between lip service and divine service, and so this week he sent out word: all the support staff in the administrative offices are invited to leave their offices and come to Chapel every morning. Offices will close.

It's a fiendishly clever plan—when the support staff leaves, the administrators, totally unsupported, will either need to do our own work or come to Chapel, too. It's a small beginning that lays hold of a great hope—for our communal lives but for the lives of each of us as questing believers—I will sing praise with the spirit.

I have long suspected that when it comes to understanding the story of Mary and Martha that was also read this morning we focus too much on the details of the story and not on its challenge. It is not necessarily a story about being in the kitchen versus being in the parlor. It's a story about being worried and distracted about many things and forgetting the one thing needful. Some of us are so worried and distracted by the syllabus that we have forgotten the hymn book; so bent on getting to the library that we dash past the Chapel. Oh, I know you're here this morning, but our time has just begun. If your mind drives you; take time for the Spirit.

II

"I will sing praise with the spirit, but I will sing praise with the mind also."

Of course Paul had another worry besides the worry that some Corinthians would be all words and no music; he had the worry that some Corinthians would be all music and no words. So full of the Spirit that they couldn't say one articulate thing about life, or their lives, or their faith, or anything else that mattered. His fear was that when it came time to pray they'd just say: "Amen, Yes Jesus." and when it came time to sing they'd just yodel. So he wrote them these strong words: "I will pray with the spirit, but I will pray with the mind also. I will sing praise with the spirit, but I will sing praise with the mind also."

If there's been a kind of theme in the opening speeches for this semester, including a couple of my own, the theme has been the intellectual love of God. Faith seeking understanding. Only yesterday as I was working on this sermon (a little late in the week, I know), only yesterday did it strike me that we have told the truth but not the whole truth about that.

The intellectual love of God is not an easy or automatic result of one's intellectual pilgrimage, not even in this place. We may make it sound as if studying the synoptic problem or puzzling about theodicy paves the smooth way to loving God with all our minds. But it ain't necessarily so. There's no telling when you start out on this quest whether it will lead you to the intellectual love of God or to the intellectual dark night of the soul. Get the faculty late at night or at coffee hour with our guards down; I'll bet most of us will tell you that the quest that may end with the intellectual love of God has also sometimes led us straight through the Valley of Despond.

Divinity School didn't hit me as hard as some, but that's mostly because college had deflated my theological confidence altogether.

My first year at college I made the mistake of taking introductory philosophy from our college's most noteworthy unbeliever. Michael Scriven was to unbelief what Billy Graham was to evangelical Christianity: fervent and persuasive. The rumor, never entirely confirmed or disconfirmed, was that Scriven had a simple grading system: A for Atheist, B for Buddhist, C for Christian, D for devout and F for Fundamentalist.

The first vacation after I started the course, I headed home and one night took a long walk with my father. "Well," I said, "Scriven has persuaded me that you can't be rational about your faith. You can be rational about astronomy and rational about economics and even rational about English literature, but you can't be rational about your faith. So when it comes to believing, I've just got to leave my mind outside the door."

"Well," said my father, "It's always seemed to me that faith is something like this. The Christian faith is like a quart jar, and there's a quart and a half of reality out there. So you can't get everything to fit, but Christianity has always seemed to me the best container we've got." It was his way of saying: have faith with your spirit, but have faith with your mind. Think about what you believe. Test your faith. See what fits.

I will sing praise with the mind. That's a daunting task, a lifelong obligation. But when you wrote Guy Martin and said you'd come study here or wrote whatever Dean and said yes, you'd work here: that's the task that you took on. And to escape it is unfaith.

The story about Martha and Mary isn't always about kitchens and living rooms. Sometimes what Martha is busy and anxious about is all the pottery and cutlery of the spiritual life. Frantically plucking her guitar or singing a happy tune without asking whether the lyrics make any sense at all. While Mary this time finds the one thing needful by heading straight for the library, notebook and pen in hand.

IV

"I will pray with the Spirit, but I will pray with the mind also. I will sing praise with the spirit, but I will sing with the mind also."

That's it, that's the covenant, that's what you've signed on for. In this place, for these years, and if it works, for all the years of your life.

A few years ago George Lindbeck retired after a long and distinguished career as a theologian at Yale. There was a reception for him in the Common Room and at the reception George made a speech. George said that some time before he'd been listening on National Public Radio to the Saint Olaf College Choir's annual Christmas concert. After the concert the announcer asked one of the choir members why she sang in the choir. "Because the choir was here before me and it will be here after I've gone," she said. "Because the music we sing was here before us, and it will still be here after we've gone."

"That's how I feel about doing theology," Lindbeck said, "I become part of a choir that began singing long before I arrived and will continue long after I've gone."

That's how we can feel about being at Yale Divinity School. Here we are part of a music that long preceded us and that will long outlast us. But for the years that we are given in this place— for the years that we are given in this place, we have the immeasurable privilege of joining our voices in the dear and blessed song.

Amen.

December 8, 1996 ·
Battell Chapel ·
Isaiah 40:1-11, Mark 1:1-8

In the following sermon, preached on the second Sunday of Advent, 1996, Dean Bartlett mentions Jerry Streets and the Slifka Center: Reverend Streets is the Chaplain of Yale University and Senior Pastor of the Church of Christ in Yale. The Slifka Center is the center for Jewish life at Yale.

Let us pray: Dear and demanding God, show us your Son. Amen.

I

It's the second Sunday of Advent, and expectation fills the air. Trees are bought or tagged, Advent lights shine in windows all around the neighborhood. At church we light our Advent candles, prepare the mitten tree and practice the pageant.

Halfway through the service we sing a not-too familiar hymn and pay some attention to words which sound as though they're going to be familiar but turn out not to be so familiar after all.

"The beginning of the good news of Jesus Christ . . ."

And since we know how that good news begins we listen for the beloved stories of angels singing and shepherds scurrying and magi searching all those miles.

But Mark, as usual, surprises us. Either he's never seen a

church pageant or he deliberately ignores the features of the story we like best.

For Mark, Gospel, good news, does not begin with the manger.

II

For Mark the good news begins with the prophet: "As it is written in the prophet Isaiah, 'See, I am sending my messenger ahead of you, who will prepare your way.'" For Mark the good news begins with what we call the Old Testament and our Jewish neighbors call Tanakh and what for Jesus and the first disciples was just plain Scripture.

And truth is, though we remember best the shepherds and the wise men, every one of our Gospels can only get underway by calling attention to the Old Testament, because truth is we can't get to the good news of Jesus in any other way.

In Luke's Gospel even before the shepherds bow there are songs sung by Mary and by Zechariah that sound just like Old Testament psalms; and the very first words that Jesus speaks when he begins his ministry are words from this same prophet, Isaiah.

In Matthew's Gospel before we get to the birth or the magi we go through the genealogy that fixes Jesus firmly in the history of Abraham and David and Rahab and Ruth.

And in the first verse of John's Gospel we hear the first verse of the Hebrew Bible. Genesis 1:1, "In the beginning God," John 1:1, "In the beginning was the word." It's hard to get what John is saying in this astonishing prologue, but if we don't know Genesis, we haven't got a clue.

One of the members of the search committee that recommended Jerry Streets as Chaplain of the University was Donald Cohen, who is head of the Child Study Center. One of the responsibilities of the committee was to travel to various churches to hear candidates preach on their home turf. Donald said that as a Jew one thing that amazed him was how much Christian worship talked about the Jews. Jews can go to the synagogue week after week and not have to talk much at all about Christians, but Christians can't get through a worship service without Israel, the prophets, the law, the promises.

Sometimes Christians worry about Judaism in ways that are wise and open, and sometimes in ways that are foolish and closed—but Donald had it right. Part of the Christian deal is that we can only understand ourselves in the light of God's dealings with Israel, and we can only understand Jesus as the Jew he was. You've read about the fuss Southern Baptists started by announcing that they would have a mission to convert the Jews. I think it's a more complicated issue than the fuss. On the one hand it's utter foolishness to think that somehow we are superior to those other children of Abraham and Sarah. On the other hand I have to admit that some of the theologians and philosophers who have most helped me understand Christianity started out their lives as practicing Jews—first among them the apostle Paul.

But in the light of this passage and in the light of the whole New Testament it behooves us to remember that in the first century the issue wasn't whether Jews could be part of God's covenant, it was whether Gentiles could. Israel's place was given—the miracle was that the rest of us were allowed to join the party. The miracle was that in the light of Jesus Christ, when we hear God speak through Isaiah, "Comfort, comfort my people," we Gentiles are actually included as part of God's people, too.

It's something to think about next time some other ugly sign of anti-Judaism appears in our community, or the next time a neighbor invites you to a Bar Mitzvah or a Bat Mitzvah, or the next time the Slifka Center has a lecture. If you want to get to Jesus Christ there is no way to get to him that does an end run around Israel. You can't really know him without the Old Testament any more than I can really know you without knowing where you came from and who your family is.

For good and honorable liturgical reasons in our worship here we stand up when the Gospel is read. More accurately, we stand up to sing a hymn and then don't sit down when the Gospel is read. There are theological traditions where that makes perfect sense.

But as a modest dissent let me remind you that the Puritans who founded this University and were the forerunners of this denomination were Calvinists, in the Reformed tradition. And for Calvinists the whole Bible was altogether and equally the word of God. No part of it more or less than any other was worthy of attention.

In that tradition we wouldn't only stand for the books called Gospels, we'd stand for the Old Testament, because that's Gospel; and we'd stand for the Epistle, because that's Gospel, too. Or, more likely, we'd sit down for all the lessons, because what you're supposed to do with the word of God is not so much honor it as to listen to it, attentively, carefully, obediently.

The beginning of the Gospel of Jesus Christ is Isaiah and Genesis and the Psalms. Thanks be to God.

III

It's the second Sunday of Advent, and expectation fills the air. Trees are bought or tagged, Advent lights shine in windows all around the neighborhood. At church we light our Advent candles, prepare the mitten tree and practice the pageant.

Halfway through the service we sing a not-too familiar hymn and pay some attention to words which sound as though they're going to be familiar but turn out not to be so familiar after all.

"The beginning of the good news of Jesus Christ . . ."

And since we know how that good news begins we listen for the beloved stories of angels singing and shepherds scurrying and magi searching all those miles.

But Mark, as usual, surprises us. Either he's never seen a church pageant or he deliberately ignores the features of the story we like best.

For Mark, Gospel, good news, does not begin with the manger.

IV

For Mark the good news begins with John the Baptist. So much less appealing than the babe in the manger—the prophet in the wilderness. Not swaddling clothes but camel's hair and a leather belt. And—worse yet—not peace on earth, goodwill among people, but John the Baptist preaches "a baptism of repentance for the forgiveness of sins."

This good news is also tough news. There is no way to get to Jesus without going through John the Baptist. No end run around the demanding prophet to get to the redeeming Christ. (Of course the redeeming Christ turns out to be pretty demanding, too, but that's another sermon.)

And again Mark is not so quirky as might first appear. Luke has the angels and the shepherds, Matthew has the magi, John has the prologue and the word made flesh—but in all four Gospels before the grown-up Jesus can give one sermon or do one miracle: there is John the Baptist. There is no way to Jesus that doesn't go through the Old Testament and there is no way to Jesus that does not stop and listen to John.

What John preaches of course is baptism of repentance for the forgiveness of sins. I will forego the temptation as a Baptist to chat with you about what that baptism might have looked like, and cut to the heart of the matter. The heart of the matter is repentance. The good news of the Gospel begins with repenting of the bad news of our lives before the Gospel came along. Christmas is not just a nice holiday to add on to the other 364 days that go on as usual. Christmas is D-Day, turning point, put off the old, put on the new, let it go, lay it down. Give it up. Repentance.

And John the Baptist stands as the stark and inescapable reminder that Christmas isn't just a matter of giving; it's a matter of giving up. Letting go whatever that old life is that keeps you from receiving the new life that comes with the incarnation of Christ our Lord.

Perhaps more than any novelist of our time, Graham Greene puzzled about sin and repentance and forgiveness. In one of his early novels, *The End of the Affair*, Greene tells the story of a woman named Sarah who is married to a man named Henry but in love with a man named Maurice. Her affair with Maurice is full of passion and delight and deceit and regret; more and more she is nagged by a vision of some fuller life that includes not only fidelity to her husband but fidelity to a God in whom she barely believes.

It's World War II; it's London. Sarah is in the hotel room waiting for Maurice. The air raid sirens, a terrible explosion. Sarah is sure that Maurice is dead. These are her words:

> I knelt down on the floor; I was mad to do such a thing; I never even had to do it as a child—my parents never believed in prayer, any more than I do. I hadn't any idea what to say. Maurice was dead. Extinct. There wasn't such a thing as a soul . . . I knelt and put my head on the bed and wished I could believe. Dear God, I said—why dear, why dear?—make me believe. I can believe. Make me, I said, I'm a fool and a fake, and I hate myself. I can't do anything of myself. *Make* me believe. I shut my eyes tight . . . and I said, I will believe. Let him be alive and I *will* believe. Give him a chance. Let him have his happiness. That wasn't enough. It doesn't hurt to believe. So I said, I love him and I'll do anything, if You'll make him alive. I said very slowly, I'll give him up forever, only let him be alive . . . and I said, people can love without seeing each other can't they; they love You all their lives without seeing You, and then he came in the door, and he was alive, and I thought, now the agony of being without him starts.

The agony of being without him, the surprising possibilities of being with God, a return to her husband, the beginnings of faith. This is the beginning of Gospel, dear friends, but it is not just a matter of happy carols and cheerful lights. The way to Bethlehem is sometimes a hard way. The way to Jesus leads through John the Baptist and the repentance of sins. That is tough news; it is good news, too.

V

At the church where we belonged in Oakland there were a number of Advent customs that we learned to love. Here is one. On the last Sunday of Advent, Christmas just about to come, two members of the choir, a soprano and an alto, sang in harmony the simple carol: "What Shall I Bring to the Babe in the Manger?"

I've lost the rest of the lyric, but I'm quite sure that what we brought were all the good gifts of our lives—our talents, our love, our faith, our hope. Bring these and lay them at the manger.

But Advent is not only about giving, it is about giving up. John the Baptizer, that scraggly, uncouth prophet stands as a constant reminder that there are other things to bring to the manger—to lay them down before the good news of God's Son.

Maybe this Advent we should bring to the manger that old jealousy that has poisoned a relationship and soured our own joy. Maybe we should lay that down. That old regret that we didn't go the other direction, all those years ago. Time to lay it down. The disappointment in someone we loved; the disappointment in ourselves; lay it down. The anger at those who did not value us as we deserved. Lay it down.

You know what it is, that damned thing you carry that can turn even the good news of Christmas into the same old blah.

Lay it down.

Christmastime is repentance time.

You can bring it all.

You can put it down.

You can leave it with the child who is strong enough to bear it all.

It's new beginning time.

Good news.

Let us pray: Dear and demanding God, here it is, all that stuff we've been carrying. Now lead us to the child. Amen.

October 30, 1997 ·
Berkeley Divinity School ·
Matthew 5, Revelation 7

Berkeley Divinity School is the Episcopal seminary affiliated with Yale Divinity School. The sermon below was preached on All Saints Day, 1997.

I

I grew up in a Baptist church with an Episcopalian minister of music. Owen Brady, the musician, openly thought it part of his mission in life to raise the tone of our music and secretly, I think, to raise the tone of our theology, too.

In those days of heroic churchpersonship we worshipped both Sunday mornings and Sunday evenings, and every Sunday evening the youth choir sang the anthem. Perhaps because it required no attempt at harmony and perhaps because he thought it mildly subversive of our Baptist ways, Owen required us on a fairly regular basis to render the hymn he loved: "I sing a song of the saints of God, patient and brave and true, they toiled and fought and lived and died for the Lord they loved and knew." Sunday evening rolls around once a week as you know and as the school year wore on Owen must have run out of ideas, because it seemed at least every other week we sang the saints song again.

Finally two members of our group, widely suspected to be my sister and myself rewrote verse one and when Owen sat down at the piano to play and conduct, we were ready. Thirty pubescent

113

voices joined in song: "We sang a song of the saints of God, we were patient and brave and true. We toiled and fought and lived and died, and now we are finally through. We sang it in April in May and in June and we'll sing it again July, and if we have to sing it once more we'll all sit down and die." The last line is a little weak, but Owen got the point.

Of course we got the point, too. As Baptists we thought we didn't have saints, but the song is subversively clever. It starts with the saints capital "S"—and one was a doctor and one was a queen and one was a shepherdess on the green. You folk will have to fill in the names on that verse. But it moves to the saints small "s." You can meet them in lanes or in shops or at tea (that Anglican note again) for the saints of God are just folk like me, and I mean to be one too.

So through the joys and trials of music we, the youth choir of First Baptist Church Los Angeles got into the business of trying to spy saints. Trying to be saints was perhaps more than we were ready to take on, but looking for them—that was a worthy occupation.

II

The Beatitudes are a wonderful guide to spotting saints. I have heard a number of worthy sermons on the Beatitudes which nonetheless got them all wrong. Turned this sheer grace into a set of laws. Law one: "Be poor in spirit so that you can have the kingdom of heaven. Be meek, so you can inherit the earth." And on and on. But Jesus isn't prescribing, he's describing. Here is what blessedness looks like. Keep your eyes open; keep your hearts open. (If the beauty of saintliness entices you to deeper fidelity, that's a bonus, but the first job is just to know it when you see it.)

Show, don't tell, our creative writing teachers told us. Jesus got there first. Show, don't tell.

"Blessed are the pure in heart for they shall see God."

Show; don't tell.

I arrived in New Haven in 1963, just after field work had turned into field education and long before it became supervised ministry. My second week on campus I went to work at Calvary Baptist Church in what is now the Yale Rep, and I stayed for four years as student minister and three more years as a member of the congregation.

It was the custom at that church for members of the Board of Deacons to meet with the minister and me for prayer before the service started, and my first Sunday on the job the minister introduced me to Georgette Darby, who was President of the Women's Society as well as a leading deacon. Georgette, as turned out to be her wont, said something surprisingly funny, and then we all tried to settle down for prayer. I discovered later that she was well known in the church for regaling Women's Society luncheons with stories that were just slightly risqué before moving on to the usual reports on White Cross bandages and rummage sales. She was a figure to be reckoned with: tall, stately, articulate, opinionated.

After I had been at the church about a month and was greeting people at the door, a shorter, quieter woman took my hand: "I'm the other Miss Darby," she said. Maybe it was because Georgette was such a leader in the church. Maybe it was because for many years Georgette had been forewoman at the Winchester Plant where they both worked, her sister's boss. Florence, greater in years, lesser in authority and presence—or so it seemed.

Before that first year at the church was out, Georgette wasn't feeling well, and the diagnosis came all too quickly. Inoperable cancer. One of my responsibilities was making a weekly round of calls to shut-ins, so every Friday I borrowed a car from one of the parishioners and made my rounds. Always I ended at 15 Osborne Street, because Georgette and Floss were there, and because they were gracious enough to be glad that I had come. Georgette kept her sense of humor to the end. One Friday afternoon, on a warm spring day, I found her sitting in the living room wrapped in a heavy blanket, shivering uncontrollably: "It's that new dance, the Watusi," she said. "I'm just trying to learn it."

She died late in the summer, and we went to Hawley Lincoln's Funeral Home at Whitney and Willow and the minister and I said what words we could say; and then we drove to the cemetery in West Haven, and there were more words, and we committed her body to the earth and her soul to Almighty God.

III

When she died, Georgette left me her car, a 1958 Plymouth, slightly larger and harder to maneuver than the Queen Mary, the final proof that it's the thought that counts and not the gift itself. Now each Friday I drove the Plymouth on my rounds ending at Floss's house, because, I told myself, I was worried about Florence, but also because we could remember Georgette together.

I was right to remember but wrong to worry. The other Miss Darby had probably been stronger all along than she let on, but now in grief and loneliness her grace and courage showed all the more.

Her gift to me when her sister died was simpler than the car—it was a copy of the New English Bible New Testament that she had given Georgette a few years before. It was inscribed: "To my dear sister Georgette, from sister Floss." To this day I do not open it without recalling the simplicity and depth of loyalty and love.

Week after week I went to visit there, and more weeks than not I left bearing two gifts—a word of encouragement, and a fresh-baked apple pie, surrounded by little wedges of foil-wrapped cheese.

There were tougher days to come. My joy in the Divinity School was followed by considerable un-joy in the graduate school, and though I had no official reason to do so any longer, I often stopped in at Florence's for conversation and a pie.

Our nation, too, had fallen on tougher days, and when I got involved in the resistance to the draft and that news made the papers and the television news, many of my parishioners were less than pleased. Floss said anyone was free to criticize me. Just not in her presence.

Not long after, I grew a beard, a dark brown version of the gray appendage I still wear. Dismay over my draft resistance paled before dismay over the beard. The Dorcas Circle of the Women's Society met at Florence's house for their monthly meeting and talk turned quickly to my decline and fall, as evidenced by my failure to shave. Florence said nothing but went to the closet where she kept her family albums. She brought down the cherished pictures of her father—a distinguished British man of the late nineteenth century. Dressed impeccably, combed impeccably, groomed impeccably—including his most conspicuous beard. End conversation.

About the end of my first year in graduate school, Florence's health began to fail, and they took her to Yale/New Haven. The gigantic Plymouth had long since stopped running, so about twice a week I took the bus from this neighborhood to the hospital. She had a hard time breathing and a hard time speaking and for once I was at a loss for words. So we held hands for a while, and then I came home.

The last day I took the bus and went to the hospital and to her room, and the bed was made and empty, and I went to find the nurse and she said: "Miss Darby expired."

A few days later we went to Hawley Lincoln's Funeral Home at Whitney and Willow and the minister and I said what words we could say; and then we drove to the cemetery in West Haven, and there were more words, and we committed her body to the earth and her soul to Almighty God.

IV

I will tell you a mystery, not the great mystery, but a little mystery that may point to the great mystery. Every so often for one reason or another I begin the day by driving Carol Bartlett to her work in Westville, and then I drive to YDS. The route from

Ramsdell Street to Prospect Street goes right by number 15 Osborne Street. There is a huge TV satellite dish sitting on the roof, but aside from that the house has not changed in the thirty years since Florence Darby died. And when I drive by, I always drive as slowly as I can.

I sing a song of the saints of God.

Show; don't tell.

"Blessed are the pure in heart, for they shall see God."

And blessed are those who love the pure in heart; we get to see God, too.

Amen.

April 10, 1998 ·
Battell Chapel ·
John 19

Good Friday 1998 was the occasion for the following sermon.

I

Notice that in John's Gospel Good Friday is not a tragedy, it's a triumph.

In Mark and Matthew's Gospel Jesus cries the awful cry of abandonment: "My God, My God, why have you forsaken me?" In John's Gospel he cries the cry of victory: "It is finished!" Which means: "I did it!"

Even the small details play the note of victory. In the other Gospels, the tired Jesus has Simon of Cyrene carry the cross up the hill. In John's Gospel the determined Jesus carries it all by himself.

In going to Calvary he does just what he wants to do, just when he intends to do it. "It is finished."

II

Louis Martyn, who lives down the road in Bethany, Connecticut, has written a lot about John's Gospel and helps us understand why this journey from Bethany in Palestine to the top of Calvary is presented without the slightest sign of Jesus' wavering, or doubting.

119

When John's Gospel was written there was a struggle going on in the synagogues of John's community. For years Jews who believed that Jesus was God's Son and Jews who doubted it had worshiped side by side—they worshiped the same God, after all, and there were all those years of shared stories, and shared aunts and uncles.

Then there was some kind of crisis, and the leaders of the synagogue decided that followers of Jesus were not good Jews after all, so they excommunicated Christians who were open, kicked them out of the synagogue.

That helps explain why some of the language about Jewish people in John's Gospel is so intemperate. It was a family feud between one group of Jews and another, and you know how it is in family feuds. The rhetoric escalates and charity goes by the board.

The synagogue crisis also helps explain why John tells the story of the crucifixion this way. Jesus is a sign of all the good that God promises to those who have the courage to confess him and follow him. Jesus is also a sign of what that courage looks like.

You may have to give up everything you've cherished to be a Christian (just as Jesus lays down his very life). But the wonder is this, that when you are willing to give up everything you will also gain everything—purpose, hope, comfort, confidence—life that is really life.

Look at Jesus; he lost it all; he found it all. The cross, which looked like defeat, was really victory. "It's finished." He cries. "I won."

III

Losing everything in order to find everything, dying to your old life in order to find a new and better life. Jesus is the great example in John's Gospel, but when John brings us to the foot of the cross, he recalls other examples, too.

There's Nicodemus. Nicodemus, a ruler of the synagogue. Top of the heap. King of the hill. CEO of the most important firm in town, or Sterling Professor of Judaica, or partner in the biggest firm. Pastor of Old First Church, Phi Beta Kappa and President of Rotary, all rolled up into one.

Nicodemus, sneaking out to see Jesus at night (because Jesus is the outsider; leader of the other party), sneaking out to see Jesus at night because there must be some promise that Jesus offers, some prize that Nicodemus can hang up on his wall with his diplomas and his honorary gavels and his picture with the Governor.

"What little thing can I add to my life to be part of your Kingdom?" he asks Jesus.

"You must be born again," says Jesus. Which is just a polite way of saying: "You've got to die." Give up all the powers and the perks and start all over again, psychologically naked as a newborn babe.

You've got to die to it all. Pull out of the synagogue which is your family and your power and your prestige and your self-esteem and cast your lot with this dubious band of believers in their risky venture.

Wander out of University Church to Zion Holiness Church or out of Yale to some Community College or out of whatever comfort makes you most comfortable to take that challenge which has absolutely nothing going for it—except the call of God.

Tell you the truth, we don't know if Nicodemus ever makes the hard choice. He pops up twice again in the story, once he shows up in time to say some vaguely commendatory things about Jesus. This is a strategy that has the advantage of not actually forcing Nicodemus to BELIEVE in Jesus, or to follow him.

And at the end—just after this cry of triumph on the cross—Nicodemus comes forward with a hundred pounds of spices to embalm Jesus. He's come halfway out of the theological closet. The one who had come to him by night now shows up in full daylight. But he still comes to embalm Jesus in the fear or the hope that if Jesus stayed dead nothing more would be asked.

My God, Jesus had asked a lot of him. It is so hard. Dying in order to find life.

IV

Losing everything in order to find everything. There is the Samaritan woman, too. If Nicodemus had to give up his distinction, she had to give up her distinctions.

Jesus is walking through Samaria, foreign territory, enemy territory. A Samaritan woman comes to the well and he asks her for a drink. She says the perfectly natural thing:

"How is it that you, a Jewish man, ask for a drink from me, a Samaritan woman?"

Perfectly natural to define ourselves over against each other. Man versus woman; Samaritan versus Jew.

Perfectly natural to take pride in being the insider, Jew, male.

But maybe equally natural to take pride in being the outsider. I know who I'm not: not a male like you, not a Jew like you. Not an oppressor like you.

Thank God we're not like the powerless say the powerful, helpless and marginalized.

Thank God we're not like the powerful, say the powerless, arrogant and bigoted.

Some of us proud to be victors and some of us proud to be victims.

Jesus marches right past the distinctions. Give me a drink from this well, he says, and I'll give you a drink from God. Give me what I need; I'll give you what you need.

He doesn't cross the line between outside and insider; he abolishes it.

The Samaritan woman doesn't give up yet. We love our distinctions we have nurtured them so long. All right, skip gender, and skip race. I'll tell you what makes us different from each other.

We worship on the mountain, you worship in Jerusalem. The rock bottom inescapable inevitable distinctions of theology. One of us has got to be right and one of us has got to be wrong. Proud

of our orthodoxy or proud of our heterodoxy. Proud of our bishops
or of our suspicion of bishops.

"Neither Jerusalem nor the mountain," says Jesus. "Neither
the creeds nor rugged individualism. Neither bishops nor just
folk."

The hour is coming, he says, when true worshipers will worship
the Father in Spirit and in Truth. The Spirit which knows no
distinctions and the Truth that does not choose sides.

You've got to die to all those splendid categories, says this
odd Jesus, in order to find your life in God.

Soon after the woman fades from sight; but before she goes,
we see her hurrying among the Samaritans, urging them to come
and see the Jew. Forgetting her own distinctions and ignoring
her own categories in order to introduce people to this amazing
life.

In her own way, dying in order to give life.

V

We don't know what had happened to the Samaritan woman
by the time Jesus came to the cross.

We do know what had happened to his mother and to the
disciple called beloved.

We do know what had happened to those two people who we
may guess loved him most powerfully and mourned him most
deeply.

There they stood at the foot of the cross as we are apt to stand
in our grief and our love.

Totally focused on the loss; totally separate from one another.

"Is there any sorrow like unto my sorrow," the mother asked
herself. The disciple asked himself.

Nurturing and cherishing what they had every right to nurture
and cherish, their exclusive, overwhelming love for the one who
was dying. Their absolute devotion to him.

And then he called them to die, too. To die to their total
attention to him and to the singularity of their grief.

"Woman," says Jesus. She looks up from her tears. He points to the disciple. "Here is your son."

"Son," he says, and the disciple must look up, too. "Here is your mother."

Demanding the hardest death of all; the death of what we have every right to. Our individual devotion and our private griefs. The awful losses that no one can take away and that no one can understand. The relationship to a beloved companion or a beloved Savior which is ours and ours alone.

Demanding that we die to that—not give it up—but transform it, transfigure it into love for the person who stands beside us. The one whose grief is not our grief but is grief just the same. The one who needs our love.

If you really love me, says Jesus to his mother. Love him, too.

If you really love me, says Jesus to his friend. Love her, too.

My God, Jesus asks so much of us. It is so hard, dying in order to find life.

VI

"It is finished!" cries Jesus. A cry of absolute victory. All is lost; all is found.

"It is finished," cries Jesus. And for him, for now it is.

But not for them, not for Nicodemus waffling, or the Samaritan woman sharing the news, or for the mother and the friend learning to make a life together.

"It is finished" cries Jesus. And for him, for now it is.

But not for us, either,

Trying to discover what pride and power we must give up if we are to be born all over again into a brand new life.

Trying to get beyond the little distinctions that give us our identity and our pride and our appalling divisions.

Trying to get beyond the absolutely valid grief and loss that keep us to ourselves, keep us from noticing that other one who grieves beside us.

His arms outstretched, his victory and loss embrace the world; even when he's crucified, especially when he's crucified, he will not let us go.

My God, he asks so much of us.

My God, he gives so much to us.

Amen.

September 18, 1998 · Yale Divinity School · Exodus 32:7-14, Luke 15:1-10

Letty Russell, mentioned in this sermon, was Professor of Theology at Yale Divinity School for many years.

I

Thirty years ago this year, on the same day, Thomas Merton and Karl Barth died.

Barth died in his sleep in Switzerland, his monumental *Dogmatics* not quite finished, but the life and the work for all practical purposes complete.

Merton died of a freak accident in Thailand, where he was still searching, most recently for ways in which Christians could learn from Buddhists, a question to which Barth devoted very little attention.

Yet the two of them in their very different ways had puzzled about a crucial question: what does it mean to be a Christian leader—for Barth, a pastor; for Merton, a priest?

Early in his career, Barth looked out the study window of his church just before the Sunday service and noticed many of his fellow townsfolk walking, not into church, but past it. He wrote, "I understand them very well. Although I think that they ought to come in and hear (me preach) about the sinners and the joy in heaven, I simply cannot tell them—and who knows if I ever will—that they must hear."

Early in his training for Holy Orders, before he was yet ordained, Merton wrote of what it would mean when at last he officiated at Mass and brought the priestly prayer. "I have been more and more impressed by the fact that it would be utterly insufficient for me as a priest to stand at the altar and pray to Christ with great personal love. Now I know there is much more. Instead of myself . . . there is the might of prayer stronger than thunder and milder than the flight of doves, rising from Christ in my soul, shaking the foundations of the universe, lifting up me, sanctuary, people, church, forest, cities, continents, seas and worlds to God and plunging everything to him."

Though it might be said that by the end of his life Barth had more and more answers to go with his questions and Merton had more and more questions to go with his answers, yet from the beginning to the end of their ministry, they represented two great gifts of Christian leadership.

Speaking of God to the people.

Praying for the people to God.

II

I am committed both in my writings and in my denominational choice to the doctrine of the priesthood of all believers. But that should not be confused with what I fear is a growing popular affection for the priesthood of no one at all. A kind of fuzzy *koinonia* where everyone takes part but no one takes responsibility.

Liturgically that makes me a little reactionary. I want someone to say, "Your sins are forgiven," not to have us all chime out together: "Our sins are forgiven."

I'd rather have the order of service say, "Leader" and "People" when it comes to the responsive sections—not just "One" and "Many." We never mean "One" and "Many" anyway. The worship planners know just which ONE is supposed to read the bits that aren't in italics. Who is supposed to read? The leader, that's who.

There's nothing wrong with having one person lead in prayer, nothing wrong with having one person lead the singing, nothing wrong with having someone lead the discussion, or lead the long range planning committee, or lead us as we think together about the Scripture, or even lead the procession down the aisle.

There may be something wrong with having the same person do all the leading every day; diversity of gifts. But in diverse ways on diverse days, we are asked to lead.

In another context on another day I want to remind all the people of God that all have the gifts of witness and intercession, that all of us are both prophets and priests. But today I want to remind you who are stuck and blessed with being leaders—clergy, teachers, directors of social ministries, music leaders—God help us actually IN CHARGE. I want to remind you, us, of the shape of our ministry.

Tell the good news of God to the people. Plead with God for the people. Like Jesus, like Moses. Prophet and priest.

III

Tell the good news. What annoys Barth is that people aren't dashing in to church to hear what he rightly believes is the best news imaginable. What he calls the news "about the sinners and the joy in heaven." Especially the joy in heaven. He might even have had our Gospel reading for this morning in mind.

In our parable Jesus tries to move the people from the heart of everyday to the heart of God. You know how a good shepherd will go chasing just one sheep? You know how a thrifty woman will search and scour for one last coin? And how they rejoice when the lost is found? Well God is that and more than that. The love that will not let you go, the joy that welcomes you home.

Whether you witness one on one, or lead an adult study class, or say a few words in the school chapel or get twenty minutes in the pulpit on Sunday morning. Here's what you do: tell them good news.

We don't know as much about politics as Doris Kearns Goodwin and we're not as funny as Jay Leno. Politics and jokes are fine. But always in the light of the Gospel. A word about God, a word about love, a word about Jesus Christ—God's love come near.

IV

Speak the good news, and pray for the people. Whether by your bed at night or at the altar—or both. Lift them up.

In our passage, Moses tries to move from the everyday to the heart of God. Moses, dare we say, appeals to God's vanity—"O Lord, what are people going to say if you bring your people out of Egypt only to slay them in the mountains?" "Think of your reputation, God." Brash, audacious, intercession.

I leave it to philosophers to try to explain how intercession works. I am a pastor, I am a friend, a spouse, a parent: I testify. Intercession is at the heart of the faithful life. Brash, audacious, intercession. "Hello, God, are you listening?"

During my first student years Kenneth Scott Latourette, the distinguished Professor Emeritus of Missions and Baptist lay leader, lived in Stuart House. He ate his meals in the Refectory, had Bible study groups in his rooms, and became friends with a great number of students.

In his pocket he carried a little black notebook, and in the notebook were the pages of his prayer list. If you indicated that you weren't feeling well, or were having trouble with classes, or if he noticed that a relationship was going sour, down went your name in the little black book.

We knew that every morning between breakfast and *The New York Times*, Latourette took time for prayer, and sometimes the names he brought to God were our names. We knew it mattered, not just in our intentions, but in God's intentions, too.

Praying, interceding. O love that will not let us go.

Pray like Moses and Merton and Latourette; witness with Jesus and Barth.

V

It's hard, even in this Christian community, not to let a little competition sneak in and muddy the *koinonia*. We're saved by grace but we're graded by works, and the grades are always more tangible.

It's hard as students not to scramble for prizes and honors.

We in the faculty are blessedly free of that worry about honors. Though I have noticed that Letty Russell's books always get review articles in the journals I read, while mine are relegated to the section called "briefly noted."

As your academic dean I always enjoy the end of the year flurry—those committee and faculty meetings when we decide who'll get the preaching prize, or the scholarship prize, or the most promising clergy prize.

As your academic dean, I am glad to help you juggle the credits and plead for the grades that will distinguish between *summa cum laude, magna cum laude* and *cum laude.*

But as a minister of Jesus Christ I remind you who you really are: servants of the servant who did not count equality with God an honor to be grasped but emptied himself for God's sake and for our sake, too.

As a minister of Jesus Christ I declare to you the honors you have already received, that the faculty can neither give nor take away.

You speak for God to the people.

You plead for the people to God.

The only honors I can promise you.

And, by God, the only honors you will ever need.

Amen.

September 23, 1998 · Berkeley Divinity School · Psalm 119:33-40, Proverbs 3:1-6, Matthew 9:9-13, 2 Timothy 3:14-17

The feast day of St. Matthew was the occasion for this sermon.

I

In all the days of my life I have only received one direct sign from heaven. It came to pass in this way.

For some time I had been the pastor of the Hyde Park Union Church in Chicago and week after week I had preached sermons that I hoped were full of the promise of the unconditional love of God.

Sunday after Sunday seated in a pew two thirds of the way to the back of the sanctuary was James Gustafson, who for many years taught Christian ethics at Yale and in those years was teaching Christian ethics at the University of Chicago. Tuesday after Tuesday, after he had given me time to recover from the anxieties of Sunday morning, Gustafson gave me his evaluation of my sermon.

On this Tuesday the evaluation was particularly pointed and clear. "What we need," he said, "is less Paul and more Matthew."

I knew exactly what he meant; all this stress on Christian freedom might have led to an undervaluing of Christian responsibility. All this justification by grace was a little short on the sanctification that came after.

Pondering Gustafson's words I wandered from the University where we had been chatting to my study in the church and somewhat abashedly decided it was time to get started on the next week's sermon.

I picked up the Revised Standard Version of the Bible that I had bought as a student some years before and started to open it on my desk, when out from the book and onto the floor fluttered seven pages. I picked up the leaves from the floor and discovered that they consisted exclusively and entirely of Paul's Epistle to the Galatians, simply worn out from overuse.

On that day I became a lectionary preacher, trying, sometimes against the grain, to make sure that Matthew got his fair time.

II

How pleased Gustafson would be to have me preaching on the texts assigned to the feast of St. Matthew. How pleased I am that the text assigned from Matthew could almost fit in Galatians: "Go and learn what this means, 'I desire mercy and not sacrifice, For I came not to call the righteous but sinners.'"

And there's Matthew himself, called to follow Jesus, not from the ranks of the righteous but from the ranks of the outcast: a tax collector, outsider, sinner. The prodigal is home, kill the fatted calf. Let's have a party. My kind of Gospel.

And yet, and yet. Gustafson's reminder nags at me still.

Matthew, in the Gospel that bears his name, isn't simply called to believe. He is called to follow. And we who have been reading through this Gospel know what following means. It means taking on all the pain and all the possibility of the Sermon on the Mount and the terrible words: "Unless your righteousness exceeds that of the scribes and the Pharisees, you will never enter the Kingdom of heaven."

Oh, Jesus comes to call the unrighteous, all right. But he calls them to righteousness.

And look at the image that Jesus uses for himself in defending his ministry to sinners: "It is not those who are well who need a physician but those who are sick."

This is not the image of the loving parent who runs down the road to greet the wayward child, or the all-accepting therapist whose only job is to listen and affirm. This is the physician who makes right what is wrong. Jesus comes to sinners, not only to affirm them—but to heal them.

III

In our other texts for this evening the Psalmist loves the law and the author of 2 Timothy loves the Scripture because law and Scripture train people in righteousness.

Not just the God who loves us but the God who leads us in the right paths.

My own guess, incidentally, is that St. Paul himself did not write 2 Timothy, it was a later Christian who, like Gustafson, thought that Galatians by itself was too inclined to set us free not only for freedom but for license. St. Paul, like St. Augustine, believed that if you loved God you could do as you chose and you'd choose just right.

The author of 2 Timothy and of the psalm (like Mr. Gustafson) have serious doubts. "Lead us in the paths of righteousness," they pray. And then they show us what the paths might look like.

Matthew's got a point; it may not be enough to forgive sinners, Christ needs to heal them, too. Christ needs to heal us, too. Lead us in the paths of righteousness.

If Matthew had written down the parable of the Prodigal Son instead of Luke, he would have added or remembered to answer another question. In Luke, Jesus makes us ask whether the elder son ever goes on into the party; Matthew would have also asked whether the younger son ever heads back to the fields.

Don't just welcome me home; lead me in the paths of righteousness.

IV

Truth is, St. Matthew will never replace St. Paul in my affections. Martin Luther said of Galatians that that Epistle was his Katherine Von Bora, a scriptural version of the woman who was his wife: his one true love.

Me, too. But Matthew has become my friend (if someone so worried about making us shape up can be considered friendly). Maybe a little bit the way Gustafson is my friend, absolutely loyal but always keeping me on my toes.

Matthew has become my friend pastorally.

Early in my ministry I had done one of my finest saved by grace sermons ending with the touching refrain: "Have you sinned? It doesn't matter, God forgives you." I am embarrassed to say I may have filled out the refrain: "Have you lied, it doesn't matter, God forgives you." "Have you cheated . . ." you can imagine the rest.

After church Thor Kommedahl who was then about as old as I am now and knew some things I didn't know about keeping a job for thirty years, and having a spouse and trying to steer your kids down some reasonably safe path, grabbed my hand and looked me straight in the eye: "I'm glad God forgives me, but it DOES matter."

Of course it matters; if it didn't matter all those years of trying to work with integrity and stay faithful to his wife and patient with his kids and unswervingly loyal to his church—that wouldn't matter. If it didn't matter Thor Kommedahl wouldn't matter. Unthinkable.

That's St. Matthew's message; Jesus comes not just to forgive our sins but to heal them. God forgives us, and it does matter.

V

St. Matthew has become my friend pastorally and my friend personally as well. I am no more ready at fifty-seven than I was at twenty-seven to say that the law saves us, but I am ready to say that the law guides us.

"Lead me in the paths of thy commandments," says the Psalmist, and the prayer avails.

I don't think Scripture gives us easy answers but I think Scripture helps us with the hard ones.

Lelia Thomasson died last year at the age of 101. Lelia Thomasson lived all her life in Missouri, in territory contested during the Civil War and in some ways contested ever since. I first met her when I was two years old and we kept in touch directly or indirectly almost to the end.

Lelia was a woman in whom faith, hope and charity lived together happily, but she inherited from her culture a kind of polite racism that got along very well with African Americans as long as they stayed in their place.

She felt a little guilty about that (she'd heard those sermons in her church for all those years about racial justice), but not much changed.

Until some people pushed for open housing in her town, and there was a ballot initiative that would open all the neighborhoods—including her neighborhood—to integrated housing.

It made her so uncomfortable; she prayed and prayed and on the morning of the vote opened her Bible to the text assigned. Proverbs 3.

> Trust in the Lord with all your heart,
> And do not rely on your own understanding.
> In all your ways acknowledge him,
> And he will make straight your paths.

So she walked straight to the polling place and voted as she knew she ought to vote and went home and began preparing for the day when she would welcome new neighbors to her neighborhood.

Jim Gustafson would have loved it; St. Matthew would have loved it. "I have come not to call the righteous but sinners."

That's the beginning. But then—wonder upon wonders— having called us sinners, Christ helps to set us right.

Amen.

May 24, 1999 · Yale Divinity School · Jeremiah 31, Mark 16:1-8, 2 Corinthians 4:1-6

The Commencement Eucharist for the class of 1999 was the setting for the following sermon. Dean Bartlett graduated with the Yale class of 1967, which he mentions.

I

"He is not here, he is risen."

The good news is also hard news. He is not here. Or more accurately, he is here only for a few more hours.

Because resurrection is resurrection, he will still be here for those of us whose jobs and commitments keep us here, but for those of you who are graduating, Christ is out of here.

So don't come back tomorrow thinking you'll find him here as he was here yesterday; and when you think on him tomorrow, don't think of him as if he belonged back here in this familiar place.

That would make the sanctuary into a tomb and confuse following him with embalming him.

Here is a sad truth. I love seeing my Yale classmates in the places God has sent them: teaching, preaching, counseling, changing lives. But I dread reunions, when the class of '67 returns *en masse*, wandering these buildings wrapped in nostalgia and driven by dismay.

They tend to remember the good old days and lose the good that is here. They remember the white, single, young men dressed in coat and tie eating dinner in the Refectory. They don't quite know what to do with the present mix or the present wardrobes. They remember daily Chapel and the occasional Lord's Supper, and they're not sure why this old Puritan place is celebrating Eucharist.

They miss the fact that the mix of gender and age and race looks far more like the whole Body of Christ than did the mix of our youth. They miss the fact that we are moving closer to being a genuinely ecumenical community. They don't know quite what to do with Berkeley or the ISM and they miss the fact that those of us who live here wouldn't know what to do without them.

Meanwhile Christ has kept marching ahead, dragging this school somewhat reluctantly in his train, but because my classmates have returned to embalm him and not to follow him, they can get confused.

Beloved, keep in touch. Come back once in a while, but not too often. Send the development office a little money, but don't plant your heart here or think that the living Christ has camped out forever in these buildings.

From now on, for you, he is not here. The good news is also hard news.

II

The hard news is also good news. He is going before you.

That is where you will see him; not here, but in those churches, schools, social service agencies, friendships, marriages, partnerships, hopes and disappointments where you head next. He is going before you.

He is going before you "as he told you." I've preached this text at least once every three years for thirty years, but this is the first time I noticed how important that is. "As he told you . . ."

In Mark's Gospel Jesus is the one who is absolutely faithful; he makes accurate predictions, he keeps his promises, he is as good as his word.

Forgive my own nostalgic moment. Thirty-two years ago when my class stood on the Quad and prepared to receive our diploma, the Dean, Robert Clyde Johnson, gave his deanly charge.

He quoted Romans entirely out of context and entirely appropriately: "For the gifts and the call are irrevocable," he said. Irrevocable.

I suspect almost none of us who stood there that day are now where we thought we would be thirty-two years later.

Thirty-two years from now you will be in the most surprising places, having traveled by the most surprising routes. But your call is irrevocable. No one will ever take it back.

He is going before you as he told you. The promises that brought you here do not, will not desert you. The one who makes the promise does not, will not desert you. Your call may lead you in odd directions; your future may look strikingly unlike your present. But he still calls you and still promises to lead.

III

The young man speaking to the women does give us one important clue about that future Christ has promised. "Jesus of Nazareth, the crucified one, is risen. He is not here."

The crucified one is risen; he leads us, but he leads us still bearing his wounds. He leads us into a future still marked and marred by suffering.

Above all other Gospels, Mark is always worried lest we turn the Gospel of the cross into a Gospel of glory: quick answers, easy success, upward and onward. "Take up your cross," Jesus says in Mark, and then in different words says it again and again and again.

Dietrich Bonhoeffer put it powerfully for his time: "We are called to join in the sufferings of God at the hands of a godless world."

But after my years of much less heroic service I am less struck by the world's godlessness and more struck by its pain. Perhaps for now we are called to join in the sufferings of God in the midst of a suffering world. We proclaim the one who is risen and among us, but risen and among us as the one who suffers for us.

The old word, still the true word, the inescapable word.

> When I survey the wondrous cross
> On which the prince of glory died,
> My richest gain I count but loss,
> And pour contempt on all my pride.

Brian Wren, perhaps my favorite of contemporary hymn writers catches what Resurrection means for Mark:

> Not throned afar, remotely high, untouched, unmoved
>   by human pains,
> But daily in the midst of life, our Savior in the Godhead
>   reigns.
> In every insult rift and war, where color, scorn or wealth
>   divide,
> He suffers still, yet loves the more, and lives—though
>   ever crucified.

IV

"The crucified one is risen," says the young man to the women. "Tell the disciples that he is going before you as he promised." Then seized with amazement and fear, the women fall silent, and Mark's Gospel falls silent, too. It breaks off, not just in mid story, but in mid sentence. Unfinished.

Those of us who rushed through Mark's Gospel in class this semester noticed that the title of this book might be "The good news of Jesus, Messiah Son of God." In that case Mark opens his book by saying, this is the beginning of my book about the good news."

But the title might also be "The beginning of the good news

of Jesus, Messiah Son of God." In which case Mark is saying: this isn't the Gospel, it's just the beginning of the Gospel.

And the book stops in mid sentence because if it came to a full stop we might think that the story was over, and we could keep Jesus back there in the story and not where he belongs, always ahead of us, leading us on.

The beginning of the Gospel of Jesus, Messiah, Son of God. Mark 1:1 through Mark 16:8—beginning, and then over to the women, over to the disciples, over to us to carry on.

Your years here, not your theological education, but the beginning of your theological education. Time to move on.

Your time here, maybe not the beginning of the Gospel, but certainly not the end of the Gospel either. At best a crucial stopping point along the way. Time to move on.

With sons fresh home from college I get my yearly chance to try to catch a little of the current slang. Have you noticed one familiar dialogue?

One person tells another some astonishing news, makes some scarcely believable claim.

The other shake a head and replies: "Get outta here."

"My Dad promised me a new car." "Get outta here!"

"Marjorie says she'll date only me." "Get outta here!"

I suppose "Get outta here" means what we used to mean by "You've got to be kidding."

But maybe when the news is truly astonishing "get outta here" means something more, too. "If what you say is true, why are you standing around? There's news to be shared; there's work to be done."

"Get outta here."

Beloved, on this blessed day there is good news.

We are immensely proud of you.

And there is better news.

We trust you to live out your call.

And there is the best news of all: Christ is not here, he is risen. He is going before you.

Now get outta here.

Amen.

October 20, 1999 ·
Berkeley Divinity School ·
Isaiah 45:1-7,
Matthew 22:15-22, 1
Thessalonians 1:1-10

I

I have been teaching preaching on and off for many years, and after extensive field research I have concluded that generations of students remember two—and maybe only two—of my basic principles.

The first principle: every sermon preaches the Gospel. What we proclaim is good news.

The second principle: good sermons attend to one or at most two texts. Juggling three is almost always an invitation to disaster.

I know that people hear this second principle, because within very recent memory I have heard Marilyn Adams, who follows me in the basic lecture course, assure students that while one text may be good enough for Baptists, Episcopalians ought to rejoice in preaching at least three.

And just a couple of weeks ago, one of your fellow students, Nicholas Beasley, began a fine sermon by warning the congregation that he was about to break Bartlett's second rule in their very hearing.

Now here I am somewhat apologetically putting my own

principles to the test. Will this sermon preach good news? I hope so; stay tuned.

Will the sermon stick to one text? Alas, no. For once the mix was just too enticing. Matthew at the center, to be sure; but then I couldn't help noticing how Isaiah on the one hand, and Paul on the other, help us think about what Jesus says in Matthew's Gospel.

II

"Christ is the answer" said all those bumper stickers of a few years ago. My guess is most of us did not have to wait for Yale Divinity School to discover that often Christ is the question, too. And in Matthew's Gospel, often the questioner.

"Should we pay the tax or not?" A tricky question. Answered by a tricky counter question: "Show me a coin, whose head is on the coin?"

"Caesar's." they say (so much more dramatic punch than the NRSV's "the emperor's").

"Give Caesar what belongs to Caesar," says Jesus. "Give God what belongs to God."

Don't let the syntax fool you. That's a question posing as a statement. Or it's an answer to the easy question "Go ahead pay the temple tax," but it raises a harder question: "All right, not in the easy case, but in the tough cases, what belongs to Caesar and what belongs to God?"

Jesus looks right past the Pharisees and straight at us. "What belongs to God and what belongs to Caesar?" And with the question, the implicit demand: "Well, for God's sake, think about it."

III

For God's sake, think about it. Not easy, but necessary Christian discipline.

The other two texts help by laying out some options, some limits, if you will.

On the one hand, Isaiah reminds us, politics and power are not in themselves evil.

> Thus says the Lord to Cyrus, his anointed—
> whose right hand I have grasped to subdue nations before
>   him—
> I will go before you and level the mountains.

Look at that. Cyrus this Persian politico, is (you all remember this from OT Interpretation) God's anointed, God's Messiah—the instrument of God's will.

(Can we notice in an aside what the text doesn't say about Cyrus? It doesn't say that he's a born again believer; he's almost certainly not. It doesn't, alas, say much about his family life and certainly not about his family values. It just says that he does what God needs him to do, and in that sense he's worthy of honor.)

It's kind of an Episcopal warning against Anabaptist sectarianism. Don't run away from government and institutions and structures as if they were all of the devil. Sometimes God has anointed the powers that be to be God's own powers.

On the other hand, Paul issues a blessedly Anabaptist warning against the dangers of loving every Caesar unhesitatingly, a warning dare we say against an undue affection for anybody dressed in purple. "All over Macedonia and Achaia people say what wonderful Christians you are—because—you turned to God from idols, to serve a living and true God." And certainly among the idols Christians had to leave aside were Caesar and his minions, too.

On the one hand, on the other.

Give Caesar Caesar's due, in the right circumstances God can make kings and emperors and deans and bishops useful.

Give God God's due: under no circumstances, none, are kings or emperors or deans or bishops worthy of unquestioning homage.

When you meet power face to face, nod your head if you must, but for Christ's sake, don't bend the knee.

IV

Think about it. What belongs to God and what belongs to Caesar? Where do we acknowledge God's right to use powers and principalities and where do we say an unshakeable "No" to idolatry?

I wish we thought about that more around here. I wish we thought about that more. Because I think it's a more central question than say, what's happening to the Quad or what's happening to the Prayer Book.

John 3:16, that much abused but inescapable statement of the Gospel says it loud and clear: "God so loved the world that God gave God's son," not, as we sometimes think, "God so loved the church."

We are so churchy here, by definition, vocation and pension plan, that we forget that God in Christ was asking us questions, not very often about church order, and very often about our responsibility for the orders of this world.

Convocation and reunion are over; all those aging alums remembering how it used to be. Indulge me for two minutes.

When I got here Richard Niebuhr had just died and Robert Calhoun was teaching still; one a so-called realist, one a real pacifist. Good friends who spent World War II arguing about what one owed God and what one owed Caesar.

And all my years as a student the war in Vietnam raged and the war on poverty, and the civil rights movement and people of good will had different opinions, but the one thing you could not do was turn a blind eye or a deaf ear and think only about what God had done in Judah or Galilee or Nicea without asking what God was doing in Washington and Saigon and Selma.

All the issues are more quiet and polite now. Gentle imperialism, genteel exploitation, racism behind closed doors.

But God is still God, and sometimes the powers that be serve God's rule, and sometimes the powers that be think they ARE God, and we had better think about it. Hard.

V

Look at a coin, says Jesus, whose image do you see? Caesar's, they say.

Look in a mirror, says Paul in a passage more famous than this from Thessalonians, However dimly, whose image do you see? God's of course. Coins made in the image of Caesar; you made in the image of God.

Give Caesar Caesar's due; sometimes a little, sometimes a lot. Not easy to know.

Give God God's due. Yourself, God's own image. God minted— minted in you. Always, everything. Not easy to do.

In that war where Richard Niebuhr and Robert Calhoun argued about what was owed Caesar and what was owed God, both of them would have admitted that their struggle was nothing compared to that of the young teacher at Union Seminary in New York.

He'd come from Germany, watched as the German churches slipped from deference to idolatry. What did he owe Caesar? What did he owe God?

So back to Germany, not only to Germany but to the resistance, and to prison, and eventually to execution.

Just before the execution, Bonhoeffer wrote the words that call us back to Christ, God's question and God's questioner, the words that call us to ourselves:

> Who am I? They often tell me
> I step from my cell's confinement
> Calmly, cheerfully, firmly,
> Like a squire from his country-house.
> Who am I? They often tell me . . .
> I bear the days of misfortune
> Equably, smilingly, proudly,
> Like one accustomed to win.
> Am I then really all that which other men tell of?
> Or am I only what I myself know of myself,

Restless and longing and sick, like a bird in the cage . . .
Weary and empty at praying, and thinking, at making
Faint and ready to say farewell to it all.
Who am I? This or the other?
Am I one person today and tomorrow another?
. . . Or is it something within me still like a beaten army
Fleeing in disorder from victory already achieved?

Who am I? They mock me, these lonely questions of
  mine.
Whoever I am, thou knowest, O God, I am thine.

Amen.

December 8, 2000 ·
Yale Divinity School ·
Luke 3:1-6, Philippians 1:3-11

The following sermon was preached during the second week of Advent, 2000.

I

Long years ago I arrived at this place as a student convinced that the theologians I least admired were St. Paul, John Calvin and Karl Barth. Some time later I wandered out into the larger world indebted to many for much—but intellectually above all to St. Paul, John Calvin, and Karl Barth.

For more than fifty years Barth kept above his study desk a reproduction of an altarpiece painting by Matthias Grunewald. At the center of the painting is the crucified Christ, and at his side stands John the Baptist, pointing. Pointing at the body of the crucified.

"That's what it is to be a preacher," Barth used to say. "That's what it is to be a theologian. John the Baptist, pointing."

Advent begins and it is time for John to point again. What do we as preachers and theologians point to this Advent?

I have preached dozens of Advent sermons through the years and I have heard hundreds. There are many wonderful truths to present at this season, but this year let me dare to suggest a couple. I'll use the old strategy of telling you what I wouldn't preach on before I tell you what I would. Not one word of this is to be taken as a criticism of the many find Advent sermons I have heard from many fine preachers sitting here this morning.

II

This Advent I'd not preach Jesus' second coming but his first. Or at least not just his second coming but also his first. I suggest this not just because it is so difficult to say anything very comprehensible about the second coming. I say this because my sense is that for this season, at least, the first coming is stumbling block enough.

Luke says that John comes to prepare the way of the Lord, and in the first instance that means prepare the way of the Lord who not that long ago had come as a baby and who is about to come as a teacher and healer and trouble-maker. Whatever it means to say that Jesus will come at the end of time, what will come at the end of time will be Jesus, this fragile child, this controversial preacher, this crucified Messiah.

So let's not berate our people for overvaluing the manger and undervaluing the parousia. If we get everybody to the manger full of expectation, hope and longing, we will have done exceedingly well.

Let's not wag our heads or shake our fingers if we find people humming "Joy to the World" instead of "Lo, He Comes on Clouds Appearing."

I once took a cross country train ride with a four year old who sang "Joy to the World" most of the way, and it was the middle of July. I had the good sense not to tell him that he was liturgically inappropriate, and I will tell you a great mystery, at twenty-one he still thinks the world is full of joy.

Karl Barth, with whom we began, wrote a good deal about last things. But the last thing he had to say, in a radio address just before he died, was this: "The last word I have to say is not a term like 'grace' but a name. 'Jesus Christ.' HE is grace, and he IS the last, beyond the world and beyond the church . . . everything that I have tested in my life, in weakness and in foolishness, is there (in him)."

III

And this Advent let's not preach one more polemical sermon on the sad materialism of American Christmas. I know, we all spend too much and eat too much—and there are huge issues of social justice of which Christmas consumption is only one symptom.

But when Luke tells us about John the Baptist, who points to Jesus, Luke lands John in the midst of material history with actual rulers and messy politics.

And when John wants people to change their lives, it's their lives he wants changed, not their souls. In the verses just after this morning's lesson, John tells people what to do with their clothing and their money. And when they repent he grabs their actual bodies and dumps them in a real river with a real splash and brings them up soaking wet.

Luke, telling us what John the Baptist points to, Luke says that John points to the one who is coming so that "all flesh shall see the salvation of God." All flesh.

Flesh is what Christ comes to redeem, not to avoid. And if the danger of our culture is that we'll make Advent too material, the danger of our preaching is that we'll make Advent too spiritual, as if Christ comes to the church and not to the world; simply recluses himself from wrapping paper, feasts and families.

A couple of years ago there were terrible floods in South Dakota, and the television reporter was interviewing the editor of the local paper. Everyone who worked for the paper had escaped the floods, but the files full of years and years of old newspapers were destroyed. The editor was just trying to assure himself that the loss wasn't as bad as it felt.

"After all," he said. "It was just stuff." And then he began to cry.

Stuff. All those years and all those memories. Stuff.

The wrong present given for the right reason. The sweater that doesn't fit because once again they got your size wrong.

Stuff.

The annual family meal that barely works, but only as long as you don't mention the election.

Stuff.

Putting the excited children to bed.

Stuff.

Laying the child in a manger.

Stuff.

The beloved body that you sleep beside at night. The body that you are. The body on the cross.

Stuff.

Baby stuck in a barn; man stuck on a tree.

Stuff.

Body broken and blood shed.

Stuff.

Bread shared and wine poured.

Stuff. Just stuff. Such stuff.

Amen.

August 28, 2001 ·
Yale Divinity School ·
Mark 1:1-8, Hebrews 11:32-12:1

Yale Divinity School's Before the Fall Orientation was the occasion for this sermon. The renovations to the Divinity School's buildings around the Quad were underway, and only one section of the new building had opened. Dean Rebecca Chopp had just begun as Dean of the Divinity School, and the University was in the midst of its Tercentennial celebrations. In this sermon, Dean Bartlett refers to the pulpit in Marquand Chapel, which is raised above the floor of the Chapel, and the fact that most of the preaching is now done from the floor as opposed to the high pulpit.

I

Every year at this time we mark a new beginning, but this year we really mark a new beginning:

New Dean.

Newly refurbished buildings.

And of course: you.

One thing I learned when I took a course in creative writing and one thing I teach when I teach preaching is this: begin at the beginning. If you've got a story to tell, just start telling it where the story begins. Don't hem; don't haw; and don't give an elaborate prologue on why you're telling the story you're telling, just begin.

But of course the Gospels never do that. Whoever else he is, Jesus is the hero of the Gospel stories, and you'd think that they would just begin at the beginning of his story. But they never do.

Matthew begins with genealogy—the long list of forefathers and foremothers, the family tree from which springs the stem of Jesse, Jesus, Lord and Savior.

Luke begins with Elizabeth and Zechariah before he ever gets to John the Baptist, and well before he gets to Jesus.

John of course trumps them both and begins at THE beginning, just as the first word of creation is spoken and the first light shines in the encompassing dark.

Even Mark, who seems to tell the most straightforward story, names Jesus in the title of his work, but then takes eight verses before he brings his hero onto the stage.

Even in Mark's Gospel Jesus is twice foreshadowed, twice heralded—by John the Baptist, who foretells Jesus, and then even farther back, by Isaiah who foretells John the Baptist.

Even in Mark's sparse Gospel our Lord is preceded and surrounded by a minimalist cloud of witnesses.

II

Whatever else may happen to us in our lives, all of us hope to be the hero or heroine of our own story. And while we know that our story does not begin in this place on this day, we like to think that a new chapter does. We'll title it "The Yale Years" or "My Search for God" or at the very least, "The Academic Year 2001-2002."

But if Jesus' story cannot be told apart from history, if we cannot begin at the beginning with him, then we surely can't begin the story with us. The history of God's people, of Israel and the Church, does not begin with our call, or our first recital, or our trial lecture, or the first article we published, and that Gospel history will not end with us, either.

And of course Yale Divinity School does not begin its life today; that's obvious when we stop to think about it, and the fact that this year Yale celebrates three hundred years of training ministers and teachers means that we won't have to work very hard to get the message. The witnesses were here long before us, and they will be here long after we have gone, teaching and learning and writing and singing.

III

I have pondered that this week, our being foreshadowed and surrounded. I have been recalling our orientation as students thirty-nine years ago. As I remember it we did not have days of orientation, but we did have tea with the faculty, and then we all marched into the Refectory where Professor Roland Bainton took us on a tour of the room, pointing out the portraits of the saints who had gone before and telling us their stories. Now Bainton's portrait hangs on the walls, too, or will again when the redecorating is done.

I also ponder our being grounded in history whenever I worship in this Chapel and especially whenever I preach. I came here first as a student in 1963 and back as a faculty member in 1990, and it came as something of a shock to me to discover that in the late 20th century and so far in the early 21st we usually preach and hear sermons from this floor level pulpit. Liturgically there is much to commend this closeness, this sharing, on the whole I affirm it.

But the low pulpit jars against my memory of sermons delivered years ago by my mentors from that high pulpit that stands behind me. Let two memories stand for a host: Julian Hartt preached a sermon on the laywoman in the church of his youth who had nurtured him to faith, and reminded us that Incarnation is not only a word to be spoken about the first century.

Brevard Childs has given his life to affirming the deep theological underpinnings of the Old Testament, but I remember a sermon he preached on the book of Proverbs and how wisdom literature might help us think about sexual ethics. It's not always a matter of Thus says the Lord, said Mr. Childs, or God was in Christ, sometimes the text just says: "Don't be stupid."

James Dittes, who teaches here still took the story of Lazarus in John's Gospel, focused on Martha's need to be freed from her excessive anxieties, and closed his sermon with Jesus' word at the tomb—a word to Lazarus, a word to Martha, and a word to the excessively busy and anxious congregation: "Free him, and let him go."

The high pulpit built in the 1930s was a reminder to the students of the fervently egalitarian 1960s of a truth from the 1630s. In Puritan worship, in which this University was born, the word of God as read and preached is held up high. Not as some alien authority to hit us over the head, but as a light to show the way.

And in the old days when we made the preacher stand up there we held her or him in high regard, not necessarily as the greatest scholar or the truest saint, but as one who was unashamed to bear witness to the light.

There is much to be said for this more egalitarian pulpit, this more familiar word, and much much to be said for a student body not so thoroughly Calvinist in its background as we were from the 17th century through most of the 20th. But my hope is that when we preach and worship here, we affirm that this friendly pulpit is backed by that high pulpit and by the faith and hope it represents.

IV

Others will speak far more knowledgeably than I about the Anglican heritage that was deepened by the coming of Berkeley to this community. Even in the more exclusively congregational years of the 1960s, one of our campus houses was named for Bishop Seabury, so that perhaps the builders of this place foresaw better and more ecumenical things to come. And while my fading memory of college philosophy courses suggests that Bishop

Berkeley thought that we were all ideas in the mind of God, it should be quite clear perhaps especially to Episcopalians, that God had many good ideas before God got to us.

V

As we sit here a little nervously, we are surrounded. Not just surrounded by the other people sitting here a little nervously. We are surrounded by the memory of the past and the promise of the future. By an institution and a cause which, however modest, is still richer and deeper than our own career alone. By those other heroes and heroines of their own stories who have gone before us and who will follow in our way.

The story never begins at the beginning. We are foreshadowed and surrounded by a cloud of witnesses, famous and anonymous, participants in a drama we did not initiate and which we will not finish.

A few years ago George Lindbeck, who had been my teacher and then years later my colleague, retired. And we held a celebratory farewell reception in the old Common Room.

Professor Lindbeck gave the closing remarks, and he told of having listened to the St. Olaf College Choir give its Christmas concert and of an interview afterwards with one of the singers. "What I like best," she said, "is that when you join this choir you become part of a song that began long before you arrived here and will continue long after you have gone."

Here, too, the song precedes our coming and will continue long after we have gone. In the midst of our search for our own education or vocation or publication or promotion, pray God we may sometimes stop to honor this place, to enjoy the song, and to join our voices to the blessed choir.

Amen.

October 7, 2001 ·
Yale Divinity School ·
Habakkuk 1:1-4, 2:1-4,
Luke 17:5-10

This sermon is reprinted with the permission of Yale University Press. Dean Bartlett offered this sermon as part of Yale's Tercentennial celebrations, less than one month after the terrorist attacks of September 11, 2001. Professor Margaret Farley, mentioned in this sermon, is Gilbert L. Stark Professor of Christian Ethics at YDS.

I

The prophet cried his anguished complaint twenty-seven hundred years go, but it could just as well have been twenty-seven days ago.

> O Lord, how long shall I cry for help
> And will you not listen?
> Or cry to you "violence!" and you will not save . . .
> Destruction and violence are before me
> Strife and contention arise.

Then after long anguish and short silence, the Lord finally replies:

> There is a vision for my appointed time
> If it seems to tarry, wait for it;

It will surely come, it will not delay;
In the meantime the one who lives right will live by faith.

Centuries later, Jesus' disciples trying hard to live right themselves have got the message—the righteous ones will live by faith—but do they have the faith?

"The apostles said to Jesus, "Increase our faith!" The Lord replied 'If you have faith the size of a mustard seed, you could say to this mulberry tree, 'be uprooted and planted in the sea' and it would obey you.'"

The grammar is a little complicated, but I think what Jesus is saying is not: "If only you had faith the size of a little seed you could move a big tree," I think he's saying: "Since you have faith the size of a mustard seed, you can move a big tree."

And how does he know that the apostles have any faith at all, even a mustard seed's worth? Because they ask for more faith. Asking for faith is the beginning of faith; the hope for faith is the birth of faith.

I drove here to church three weeks ago to a nearly full Chapel, past all kinds of churches full to overflowing. At Yom Kippur a few days later, the streets around our local temple had cars parked everywhere. Attendance at mosques all over the nation rose markedly. Of course fear brought us there but also faith: maybe the hope for faith or the memory of faith, but faith.

Look at us here this morning. Of course it's a special celebration for academy and community alike. But there have been more than enough other events this weekend to show our civil loyalties. We didn't need to squeeze this worship in between the fireworks and the football. Loyalty brought us here but also faith: maybe the hope for faith or the memory of faith, but faith.

Here's the surprising word Jesus speaks to his apostles. A little faith is faith enough to make the most astonishing change. Nascent faith and vestigial faith are still faith. If you ask for faith nervously or remember faith faintly, you're on your way.

II

Therefore this sermon does not demand faith or even recommend faith; it just assumes faith. Given that we're all here with at least a mustard seed's worth of faith, how might we live in this time of celebration for our school and anxiety for our nation?

First, faith hopes in a vision. God tells Habakkuk to stand like a watchman in the time of terror and hope steadfastly for the vision of God to do what's right.

Stand with your mustard seed worth of faith and hope for the vision to come.

Those clergy who founded a little college in a little colony with whatever faith they could muster that day hoped for a vision, and have received I dare say far more than they could have imagined. There is plenty of talk about Yale's heritage and greatness and influence this weekend. And Habakkuk before recommending faith warns against pride. So put it simply: that modest beginning, sown in hope, brought forth this University we love.

Rosa Parks, whom we honor with a lectureship at the Divinity School each year, refused to move to the back of that Montgomery bus because she bore an unquenchable hope and because she was tired. Martin Luther King found the words to affirm Rosa Parks' vision in sermons from this pulpit and around the nation: "The moral arc of the universe bends toward justice," he said. We are far, far from where we need to be in dealing with racism in this nation, but we are also far from where we were.

> There is a vision for the appointed time
> If it seems to tarry, wait for it.
> It will surely come; it will not delay
> And for now, the righteous will live by faith.

A mustard seed of faith helps us live in hope in the light of September 11, as well. The cover of *Newsweek* this week asks in

bold letters: "How Scared Should You Be?" I don't know about
you, but I've never needed lessons in anxiety.

How faithful can we be? That's the more pertinent question.
We can take the mustard seed of hope, and we can live faithfully.
We can learn from peoples who live daily with the embattlement
we've only experienced this past month. Go to work; go to church
or synagogue or mosque; celebrate holidays and tercentennials.
Hold firm the rights and liberties that give us cause to celebrate.

I like what William Safire wrote in his column on Yom Kippur:
"On top of a panicky rush to eliminate rights, too many of us are
afflicted with a 'nameless, unreasoning, and unjustified terror.'

"We'll shake off that dread. Americans will return to our
future's normalcy . . . Our children's world will be rightside up.

"I believe that especially" said Safire, "on this somber Day
of Atonement as Jews ask God to seal their names in a symbolic
book. It is not a book of fear or lamentation. In an ageless
affirmation of hope, we call it the Book of Life."

The righteous will live by faith.

III

Faith hopes in a vision, and faith seeks reconciliation.

The verses from Luke's Gospel that come just before the
passage that we heard help us understand why the apostles are
worried about the state of their faith.

Jesus is talking about forgiveness, "If your brother or sister
sins against you and repents, you must forgive. And if that same
person sins against you seven times a day and says, 'I repent'
you must forgive."

Then, just then, the disciples say: "(Yikes) increase our faith."

Of course increase our faith. It takes faith to forgive another
the wrongs done against us. It takes faith to believe that our
forgiving will make a difference. It takes enormous moral courage
to be willing to risk being wronged again. But I have absolutely
no doubt that in the personal world of which Jesus was speaking—

of family, neighborhood, faith community—the faith that risks forgiveness is the faith that increases righteousness.

It is so much harder when we move to the larger world of nations and of politics. Surely we believe that King is right that the moral bow of the Universe is bent toward justice.

At least in domestic politics he knew what that meant: speaking to African Americans who had been wronged in so many ways, he laid his claim to the faithful life: "In the process of gaining our rightful place we must not be guilty of wrongful deeds . . . Again and again we must rise to the majestic heights of meeting physical force with soul force."

Even in the face of international terrorism we seek to live by faith, to live under the claim that faith points toward forgiveness between persons and reconciliation among nations. But it is very hard to know just what that means—how we live out the vision.

I confess that I stand with Professor Margaret Farley who recently told a discussion of these recent events that she wishes she could be a pacifist but she can't. I do know that the witness of radical reconciliation is absolutely essential to the health of this nation and the hope of the nations—and any attempt to silence or shame those who are steadfastly peaceful shames our nation.

There are modest things all faithful people can work for as we wait like Habakkuk for the vision of a deeper peace.

We can insist that we have the same standards for international justice that we insist on at home: that we base justice on evidence; that we do not unilaterally serve as victim, jury, judge.

As our leaders have largely done we can resist any attempt at scapegoating, at racial or religious profiling. Fear is the breeding ground of prejudice, and faith is the enemy of fear.

And we can once again remember that a university, our University, is not merely a spectator in the great movements of history. Issues of justice, proportionality, equity, religious difference, economic growth, conflict resolution are the stuff we talk about day by day. We are allowed, invited, challenged to make sure that we become part of the public discourse, too.

There is a table set before us here for world communion Sunday. Talk about mustard seeds. Who would have believed that a sad farewell meal among a small group of friends would begin a table fellowship that has extended through two millennia and spread across the earth?

This table is one vision: a vision of reconciliation among all Christian peoples. Even that vision is not yet complete. Not all Christians are yet willing to come to the table.

But the table is also a sign of an even larger vision: of a neighborhood larger than the Christian neighborhood and a guest list long enough for all the earth.

We are not there yet; we will not see it while we live. But there is a vision for the appointed time. It will come; it will not forever delay. And meanwhile, for now, the righteous live by faith.

IV

Most of us have been at Yale's Commencement, either regularly or from time to time.

Commencements remind us of our heritage, not only the splendid combination of informality and pomp—little jungles on the mortarboards of Forestry and Environmental Studies students; the President speaking in Latin to award the PhDs. Commencement is also the odd combination of a pluralistic research University rooted in a religious college. That heritage is evident in the prayers, but perhaps especially in the hymns we always sing—one written at the dedication of the first Yale building in New Haven; the other written for the bicentennial of our city in 1838.

I have noticed that when Tom Duffy and the University Band begin to play the last hymn, the singing, at least in my section of the audience, is a little thin.

> O God beneath thy guiding hand
> Our exiled fathers crossed the sea
> And when they trod the wintry strand
> With prayer and psalm they worshipped thee.

Perhaps both words and tune have simply faded from memory, or perhaps we remember more clearly in the 21st century than they did in the 19th that some of our exiled fathers and mothers came to this country on slave ships; and some of our fathers and mothers got exiled only when the Puritans and their friends arrived on these shores.

But as the music continues all of us remember, not just the tune but the heritage—recalling the faith with which this city and this University began: faith sometimes as small as a mustard seed, faith that does ransom hope from terror and reconciliation from hate. Faith that stands strong as a watchman against the threatening night.

And the singing swells and grows:

> And here thy name, O God of love,
> Our children's children shall adore
> Till these eternal hills remove
> And spring adorns the earth no more.

"Amen," we sing.
Amen.

November 1, 2001 ·
Yale Divinity School ·
Matthew 5:1-13

All Saints Day was the occasion for this sermon, which Dean Bartlett preached on Prospective Students Day at Yale Divinity School. Professor Margot Fassler, mentioned in this sermon, was the Director of the Institute of Sacred Music and is Robert Tangeman Professor of Music History and Liturgy. She is a Roman Catholic.

I

One of the things that I love about this school is its interconfessional worship. Last week a Lutheran service to prepare for reformation day, sung morning prayer on Wednesdays, a revival by the Black Seminarians tonight.

Twice in the last three years, however, our rich diversity has presented me with a particular challenge. Twice I have agreed to preach for services on November 1, always forgetting—and this will be a clue—always forgetting that November 1 is also All Saints Day.

Now here is the problem as we gather on this All Saints day—both my companionable liturgist and I are Baptists—and on the Baptist liturgical calendar, All Saints Day is not only downplayed, it is entirely invisible.

Let me be clear about my gratitude for those traditions that hold the saints in high esteem. On occasions in recent years when I have faced the kind of crisis that afflicts humankind I have been genuinely moved to open my e-mails and receive from Professor Fassler the word that she is praying for me, and the list of saints to whom she prays.

I am here to testify to the efficacy of those prayers.

But you need to know this about the Baptists. Like many other Protestants we talk a lot about the priesthood of all believers, but an even more central conviction is this: the sainthood of all believers.

We base this conviction on our commitments to being a biblical, if not a biblicist people. And as you well know, in the New Testament, "saints" is a term, not for a particular subset of Christian people, but for the whole community.

When Paul writes to the "saints" at Philippi, he's not writing to a particularly holy subset of that community—he's writing to the whole gang.

And when Paul refers to the people we think of as official saints, he has other terms for them. He does not refer to himself as Saint Paul, but as Paul the apostle, and he does not refer to Saint Peter or to Saint James but to those so-called pillars of the church at Jerusalem.

That stress on the larger meaning of "saints" reaches across denominational lines, too. However much a particular church may honor particular saints, when it comes to funeral services I have noticed we all stand and sing "For All the Saints"—not in memory of St. Anne or St. Francis in particular, but in memory of all believers, especially the believer whose loss we mourn that day.

II

So here I am wanting to say some Baptist things about All Saints Day, trusting that you will find other places and other words later in the day to hear other perspectives on sainthood.

I am helped by the text, the Beatitudes, because no one would think that these are words about a subset of believers. Those whom Paul calls the "saints" Jesus here calls "the blessed."

And blessedness is not reserved for the few, it is the promise and the hope and the responsibility of the whole community.

Blessedness, the sainthood which is the gift to all believers is both a present gift and a future promise.

The poor in spirit are blessed right now because their spirits are formed aright and they will be blessed because theirs will be the kingdom.

Those who mourn are blessed right now because only those who truly love can truly mourn and they will be blessed because they will be comforted.

And those whose hearts are pure are blessed because what could be more blessed than to have a whole heart in a divided world? And they will be blessed because—when all is said and done—they will see God.

Blessed are the pure in heart, for they shall see God. On All Saints Day we want to name our saints; reading the beatitudes we want to recall the blessed. I recall a Baptist saint who was a blessing.

A. King Boutwell was his name, and I first learned of him the summer before I came to YDS when I received a letter from him. The letter was written on stationery with a purple letterhead and it was signed with purple ink. It invited me to cheat a little on the Supervised Ministry process and to come work with King at the Calvary Baptist Church.

Calvary Baptist Church stood at Chapel and York Streets in downtown New Haven in the building that is now the Yale Repertory Theater. In his memoirs the then Dean of the Drama School wrote how ironic it was that what used to be a Baptist church was now a theater.

He thought it was ironic only because he never heard King preach. Dressed in morning coat and tie, leaving notes and pulpit behind, marching up and down the platform, leaning out over the audience to make a point, King outplayed most of the plays I have seen at the Rep since.

And his homiletic imagination rivaled the dramatic imagination of Shaw or Brecht. For instance, while Baptists do not recognize All Saints Day we do recognize Mother's Day, and one of King's challenges was to find a text that would allow him to preach a Mother's Day sermon year after year after year.

Once the sermon was called "Sisera's Mother," because, as you may remember, after the feisty Jael has driven a tent peg through Sisera's head, Deborah sings a song that pictures Sisera's mother staring out the window waiting for her son to return. She thinks to herself, "Are they not finding and dividing the spoil, a girl or two for every man, spoil of dyed stuffs for Sisera."

King drew the obvious conclusion. What caused Sisera to go wrong? This greedy mother dreaming sexual and economic exploits for her son. Thank God our Baptist mothers are not like that.

Or another year, Lazarus' mother, a woman unmentioned in holy writ. But when Lazarus died, Martha and Mary wept; a close knit family. And behind every close knit family, you got it, a Mother.

You laugh, I laugh. I laughed at the time. But notice this, after thirty five years I still remember the sermons.

I will tell you a mystery, it is essential for sermons to be biblically literate and pastorally wise—but it is not a sin that they be interesting.

III

Blessed are the pure in heart, for they shall see God.

King also collected classic cars. When I worked with him he had a 32 Lasalle and a 34 Cadillac. He loved making pastoral calls in the classic cars. He'd dress up in a tweed cap and a long scarf and a duster, and hop into his motor car, dressed a lot like Toad in the illustrations for *The Wind and the Willows*.

I was amused that he drove all over Connecticut in odd dress and old cars to call on people who were mourning, or suffering injustice, or ill. What the people remembered years later, was not how he came, but that he came.

I will tell you a mystery, preacher, or teacher, or social

worker—when people are in need it doesn't matter what you show up wearing or what you show up driving—what does matter is that you show up.

IV

Blessed are the pure in heart, for they shall see God.

I said that the first letter I received from King was printed on purple letterhead and signed with purple ink. When I came to work for him he told me that he had redesigned the church stationery so that it would be ecclesiastical purple, but I soon realized that that was just a cover for his real belief: he wrote in royal purple.

A King Boutwell told me that when he was a boy he was convinced that the "A" in his name was not an initial but the indefinite article. He wasn't A. King Boutwell, he was a king, Boutwell, exiled for a time from his Kingdom in the care of this kindly Baptist couple who raised him. One day the herald would come and summon him back to his Kingdom.

I laughed every time I thought about that in the years that we worked together, and from time to time in the long years after when we saw each other only occasionally.

I had forgotten all about that supposed royal heritage until some years later when I got the word that after his long struggle with Lou Gehrig's disease, King had died.

It happened that I was teaching the Book of Revelation that spring, and that week we had studied these words about the city of God:

"God's servants will worship him . . . and there will be no more night; they need no light of lamp or sun, for the Lord God will be their light—AND THEY will reign forever and ever."

And suddenly the young boy's dream of exile and return was not fantasy it was faith. The vision of God's consummation for King Boutwell and for all the faithful. All rulers, all kings, all saints.

Amen.

May 27, 2002 · Yale Divinity School · Genesis 1:1-13, 2 Corinthians 4:1-12

Dean Bartlett preached the following sermon at the Commencement Eucharist service for the class of 2002. This sermon was preached at a time when national news was being made about preachers who plagiarized their sermons.

I

The apostle Paul defends his ministry against his detractors: "Therefore, since it is by God's mercy that we are engaged in this ministry, we do not lose heart . . . we refuse to practice cunning or to falsify God's word; but by the open statement of the truth we commend ourselves to the conscience of everyone in the sight of God."

To get to the heart of Paul's message I turn to a novel, now some years old. The novel is called *The Final Beast*. It was written by Frederick Buechner, who was then a very young Presbyterian minister, and not surprisingly it tells the story of a young minister trying to figure out what it is he is supposed to do.

The minister's name is Roy Nicolet and he notices that a young woman named Rooney Vail sits each week quietly at the back of the church. Like a good pastor he goes to call on Rooney

169

and her husband Clem, and he's taken aback when Rooney interrupts the polite conversation with a strong reminder: "There's just one reason you know, why I come dragging in there every Sunday. I want to find out if the whole thing's true. Just *true*," she said, "that's all. Either it is, or it isn't, and that's the one question you avoid like death."

As preachers we're good at telling people that the Christian faith is pleasant, or useful, or comforting. As teachers we're good at telling students that early Christianity is historically interesting and Christian theology enticingly puzzling. But from time to time we also remember to tell them that it's true.

God was in Christ reconciling the world to God's own self.

True.

By grace you are saved through faith.

True.

Christ died for our sins.

True.

And on the third day rose from the dead.

True.

Not just nice, not just interesting. True.

And of course there's a corollary to the truth of the Gospel: it's the truth of the sermon, the truth of the lecture, the truth of our counseling. "By the open statement of the truth we commend ourselves to the conscience of everyone in the sight of God."

I wish I'd had this at hand when a few reporters called after the word was out that many a sermon came not from the heart of God or the wisdom of the preacher but from the resources of the Internet.

Phillips Brooks, in this school's most famous Beecher Lectures, said that preaching is truth through personality, and he knew that teaching was too.

That does not mean that the only effective preachers are the perkiest one. It does mean that the integrity of the word is tied to the integrity of the preacher, the value of the lesson to the honesty of the teacher.

Here's the deal: if I can't trust you to be honest about the source of your stories, I can't trust you to be honest about the source of my redemption.

We want to know if it's true; just true, that's all.

II

Paul goes on. "For it is the God who said, 'Let light shine out of darkness,' who has shone in our hearts to give the light of the knowledge of the glory of God in the face of Jesus Christ."

When the Massachusetts Bay Congregationalists founded a college in Cambridge they chose as its motto: *Veritas*. Truth. When a slightly more evangelical group of Congregationalists set up a competing college in Connecticut, the motto was also a deliberate contrast: *Lux et Veritas*. Light and truth.

The light that shone at creation and at the new creation in Jesus Christ. Not just the truth we seek but the light that illumines everyone through him.

Not just truth but saving truth.

Frederick Buechner says, when he writes his novel, that what we receive in Jesus Christ is both light and truth, saving truth. Remember Rooney Vail has told the minister Roy Nicolet is that the reason she drags into church each week is to find out if the whole thing's true, just true.

But as Nicolet stays as her minister and learns her story he learns the depth of her dissatisfactions, a kind of sorrow that led her into brief adultery and long regret.

Nicolet wonders what he ought to do, and learns quickly what every clergyperson learns. Find some layperson who knows more than you. His layperson is an older woman in the church named Lillian.

Here's what Lillian says: "Don't just give her advice, Nicolet, give her what she really needs."

"Give what, for Christ's sake?"

"She doesn't know God forgives her. That's the only power you have—to tell her that. Not just that he forgives her the poor little adultery. But the faces she can't bear to look at now. Tell her

God forgives her for being lonely and bored, for not being full of joy with a houseful of children . . . tell her that sin is forgiven because whether she knows it not, that's what she wants more than anything else—what all of us want. What on earth do you think you were ordained for?"

"For we do not proclaim ourselves, but we proclaim Jesus Christ as Lord and ourselves as your slaves for Jesus' sake. For it is the God who said, 'let light shine out of darkness,' who has shone in our hearts to give the light of the knowledge of the glory of God in the face of Jesus Christ."

III

And then the inevitable, necessary qualifier. "But we have this treasure in common clay pots, so that it may be clear that this extraordinary power belongs to God and does not come from us."

Notice how powerfully theo-centric is this claim. Our finitude, our limits, not primarily to give us humility, but to give God glory. Our vocation, our enthusiasm, our education, our prizes—not really the prize at all. Common clay pots, useful clay pots, vessels that contain the prize. The prize: the immeasurable glory of our God, the light that shone at the beginning and that now shines in our ministries so that all may see the transcendent power that belongs alone to God.

We know Bonhoeffer the hero, as much as any Christian in the last century wrestling with the obligations and the ambiguities of faithfulness. But to himself he seemed anything but heroic, an ordinary, weary man, common clay pot maybe, by God's grace, useful to God.

Let his words be our words, a poem written in prison just days before he was executed for his part in the plot against Hitler.

> Who am I? They often tell me
> I step from my cell's confinement
> Calmly, cheerfully, firmly,
> Like a squire from his country-house.

Who am I? They often tell me . . .
I bear the days of misfortune
Equably, smilingly, proudly,
Like one accustomed to win.
Am I then really all that which other men tell of?
Or am I only what I myself know of myself,
Restless and longing and sick, like a bird in the cage . . .
Weary and empty at praying, and thinking, at making
Faint and ready to say farewell to it all.

Who am I? This or the other?
Am I one person today and tomorrow another?
. . . Or is it something within me still like a beaten army
Fleeing in disorder from victory already achieved?

Who am I? They mock me, these lonely questions of mine.
Whoever I am, thou knowest, O God, I am thine.

To Christ be thanks and praise.
Amen.

September 11, 2002 · Yale Divinity School · Matthew 5:1-13

September 11, 2002, marked one year from the terrorist attacks in New York City and Washington, D.C. Dean Bartlett preached this sermon—in which he comments on President George Bush's appellation "Patriot's Day" for the day—in Marquand Chapel during a service of remembrance one year from the attacks. On September 11, 2001, the Divinity School community had gathered— led by Dean Chopp, Dean Bartlett, and Dean Dale Peterson—for hymns and prayers as news from New York and Washington, D.C. continued to unfold.

I

The Beatitudes, the blessings with which Jesus begins the Sermon on the Mount, are counterintuitive, maybe even countercultural.

Nothing is what it appears to be; the world turned upside down.

"Blessed are the peacemakers, for they will be called the children of God."

Counterintuitive. Maybe even countercultural.

The President has decided that this is "Patriot's Day." but while I do not deny the value of patriotism, that seems to name too small a thing.

We are here as a community of memory and hope, and what we remember is not just an American loss but a human one.

The immediate victims of September 11, 2001, were not just Americans but citizens of innumerable nations . . .

And what we Americans felt, some of us for the first time, was not just what it meant to be American but what it meant to be vulnerable members of the human community: no more immune to disaster than Palestinians or Israelis or Irish or Congolese.

"Patriot's Day" is too small a name for what we remember, and too small a vision for what we hope.

For many years H. Richard Niebuhr taught in this place and regularly preached in this Chapel. Here is what he wrote about the hope that drives people who are loyal to their nation but even more loyal to their God. "The power that has brought this nation into being has also elected into existence its companion nations; and the rights of such nations to life, liberty, and the pursuit of their well-being are equal in the universal commonwealth of being . . . It is not a question about our loves, but about our faith, about our ultimate confidence and our ultimate fidelity (to God)."

"Blessed are the peacemakers . . ."

II

"Blessed are the pure in heart, for they will see God."

We are a community of memory and of hope and what marks us is in large measure what we remember and what we hope for. What marks us is that we hope to see God.

Now some of you have heard me say that those of us who are believers need to attend to the daily world of our congregations and not just to the liturgical world of our communities of faith.

But now I want to say just the opposite. Those of us who are people of faith need to attend not just to the daily world of history, but to the counter-story, the counterculture, the secret history that runs alongside and underneath the obvious history.

Driving home the other night Carol Bartlett and I were

listening to yet one more of the deluge of 9/11 stories on public radio.

The streets in our neighborhood were lined with cars and the sidewalks with people as our Jewish neighbors headed to the synagogue to celebrate Rosh Hashanah, the new year, a community of memory and hope.

It is part of our memory and our hope that the eleventh day of September 2002, is also the fifth day of Tishri, in the year five thousand seven hundred and sixty-three; reminding us that God was hard at work long before we had a nation, even long before we had a church.

Remember 9/11 by all means. But broaden and deepen that memory by remembering Rosh Hashanah and Yom Kippur and Passover and Advent, Good Friday, Easter . . . that countercultural story that qualifies even our most awful or exhilarating tales. God's story.

III

"Blessed are those who mourn for they shall be comforted."

What gets us, of course, is not just the loss but the threat. Theoretically we always knew that every person is mortal and every human endeavor vulnerable, but now we know it in our bones.

What we need is comfort for our mourning and assurance against our fear.

What we need is some word that is counterintuitive, countercultural, some word that is genuinely counter-terror.

Last year on September 11 when Rebecca Chopp and Dale Peterson and I met to plan a simple service, we tried to find the words that Scripture might provide.

Not surprisingly we found the words that all of us had read and heard at funeral services for faithful people we had loved. Not surprisingly we found the words to which we turn because they are words of memory and hope.

God is our refuge and strength,
A very present help in trouble.
Therefore we will not fear, though the earth should change.
Though the mountains shake in the heart of the sea.

God is our refuge and strength.
Therefore we will not fear.
Therefore we will not fear.
Therefore.

January 31, 2003 · Yale Divinity School · Isaiah 50, Mark 6:47-52, Galatians 3

Dean Bartlett preached the following sermon during the Divinity School's All-School Conference, the theme of which was balancing academics with spirituality. Dean Dale Peterson, mentioned in this sermon, is the personable and exuberant Dean of Students at Yale Divinity School.

I

Some of you will remember the British comedy series *Monty Python's Flying Circus.* A regular feature of the program was called "The Department of Funny Walks." The actors, careful observers of the daily world in which they lived, simply acted out ways of walking they had noted on the London streets, the strut, the hobble, the circumambulation.

Inspired by Monty Python's close analysis I have long since discovered that there's such a thing as the Dale Peterson walk. Dale never goes directly from point A to point B. His perambulations are always paradigmatic of life's little detours. Of course for him the detour is always a person with a greeting, a question, a need, an anxiety.

I regret to admit that I've also noticed the David Bartlett walk, which is pretty much from here to there and straight ahead.

Nodded to I nod back and greeted I greet, but if I'm on the way to a faculty meeting or the classroom I suspect that my body language seldom suggests: "Oh, let's just stop and chat awhile."

My observations are confirmed by the strategy Dale and I have arrived at when we're headed to the same engagement. I long since gave up trying to walk together. We decide on the destination, and then I give him about a six minute lead. Unfailingly, handicap and all, somewhere between here and there I still pass him by.

In this way and in this way only I am more like our Lord than is Dean Peterson. Not only does Jesus set his face steadfastly for Jerusalem, in this passage from Mark's Gospel Jesus seems to set his feet steadfastly for the other side of the lake, even though the shortest route is across the water and not around it.

And though the disciples are in dire need of a little pastoral assistance, Jesus, driven either by his own agenda, or distracted by higher thoughts, or concentrating on not sinking, gets ready to pass them by.

II

Early this week I was trying to put together a sermon on Isaiah 50 and the remarkable claim that rightly to teach and learn is rightly to comfort and sustain. I thought that was a terrific word for a week in which we have been thinking about how intellect and spirit might come together in our life here.

Later that day Professor Kelsey said pretty much all I thought there was to say about the combination of information and formation, so I put the assigned text from Isaiah on the back burner for some other time.

Then midweek I had lunch with Professor Swancutt, a chance to catch up with each other after a fairly frantic time for each of us. She and I got to talking about a crisis in my family, the illness of our son. She told me that in times of crisis she had sometimes found faith, and I confessed to her that in this time of crisis I mostly felt fear.

But Diana's testimony comforted me and drove me to the assigned text from Mark. Here was a story about crisis, and I thought I remembered how the crisis went. Jesus, walking across the water sets out to pass the disciples by—they cry "Save us Lord!" And he turns to save. Helped by Diana's testimony I thought I'd be helped by Mark's testimony, too. If only I could learn to cry "Save, Lord," help would come.

It didn't hurt of course that in our other text, Galatians, Paul reminds us as he so often does that we are redeemed by faith.

So imagine my surprise when in that awkward moment of homiletical preparation when I actually had to read the text, I discovered that the disciples are not redeemed by faith, they are redeemed by fear. Or more accurately, of course, they are redeemed by Jesus but only because they are pretty much scared to death.

They don't cry "Save us Lord" they cry "Yikes, a ghost!" and their terror at last detours Jesus from his messianic march toward the other shore and causes him to attend. "For they all saw him and were terrified. But immediately he spoke to them and said, 'Take heart, it is I, do not be afraid.'"

III

Surprised by this story I thought I knew, I went back to see where else this Gospel I thought I knew might surprise me in much the same way.

Jesus sleeps in the bow of the boat while the seas roar and foam, and it's not faith that wakes him, it's fear: "Don't you care that we're perishing up here?" the disciples cry. Woops. Yawn. Okay. I'll attend.

On the Mount of Transfiguration what incites even God to speak is not the disciples' faith, it's their terror. As they shake in their boots the heavenly voice at last speaks out: "This is my son, the Beloved."

And as the story reaches its climax Jesus is marching steadfastly toward Jerusalem, steadfastly as he marched across the sea, and his followers are terrified because they do not know what lies ahead he tells them in no uncertain terms what lies ahead: danger, and death, and then—amazingly—redemption.

I'll tell you a mystery. For forty years I've been trying to figure out the odd last verse of Mark's Gospel, when the tomb is empty and the women hurry away, because in Mark's own words: "They went out and fled from the tomb, for terror and amazement had seized them, and they said nothing to anyone because they were afraid." End sentence. End Gospel.

"How can this be good news?" I wondered. How can this be Gospel? And sitting in Stuart house on Wednesday afternoon I finally got it: "If the women are that scared he's bound to turn up soon. He always does."

Just beyond the final conjunction and around the next corner, of course he'll be there: "Take heart; it is I. Do not be afraid."

IV

Beloved, here's the deal, he walks steadfastly and we row frantically.

Storm or no storm, he seems to be marching toward Zion whether we intend to join him or not. Some of us cry to him in faith and some of us cry to him in fear. Then oddly, graciously, he brings his relentless marching to a halt and does attend.

And sometimes, at the astonishing intersection of his determination and our terror, time stops, and he turns to us and we turn to him.

And he gives us himself, to eat and to drink.

And he says the word that calms our stormy souls: "Take heart; it is I. Do not be afraid." Amen.

May 25, 2003 ·
Yale Divinity School ·
Jeremiah 31:31-34,
Matthew 28:16-20, 2
Corinthians 3:1-6

This sermon was preached at the Commencement Eucharist service for the class of 2003.

I

The blessed St. Paul hates to boast. Boasting implies self-righteousness, works righteousness, self-sufficiency, all those things he spends his whole apostolate preaching against.

The blessed St. Paul hates to boast.

Except of course when he is driven to it.

And he is driven to it when those bothersome quasi, pseudo, ersatz, so-called super apostles ride into Corinth and question his credentials.

Apparently these so-called apostles come bearing letters of recommendation from the faculty, perhaps at St. Peter's College of Jerusalem, and it seems quite likely that they bring their resumes as well. Not only do these resumes list the super-apostles' names, degrees, and former places of apostolic employment, they slip in, ever so modestly, that enduring proof of their credentials, a word about their degree:

Master of Apostleship, *summa cum laude.*
Magna cum laude.
Cum laude.
Paul responds *Summa cum annoyance.*
"For we are not peddlers of God's word, like so many. Surely we do not need, as some do, letters of recommendation to you, or from you."

II

Christ is our recommendation, says Paul, and God is our sufficiency. "Such is the confidence that we have through Christ toward God," he writes. Not that we are competent of ourselves to claim anything as coming from us; our competence is from God."

This has been an anxious few weeks, beloved. We have seen you dash from library to computer lab, from study group to exam room, worried about grad school, worried about employment, worried about ordination.

It's only just begun.

Annoying and stress ridden as this place may be, I will tell you a sad mystery. This is the kindest, gentlest place that you will ever have to worry about how well you're doing. Grad school is tougher, the church is tougher, and all those other jobs we loosely call the real world are tougher, too.

If we had to be competent of ourselves, as Paul says in the NRSV, if we had to be sufficient, as he used to say in the RSV, then who could stand? Not one of us: *summa, magna, cum,* just grateful to get out of here alive. Not one.

Such is the confidence we have in God. Not in ourselves, not in our gifts, not even in our education. Such is the confidence we have in God. Not that we are sufficient of ourselves to claim anything as coming from us; our sufficiency is from God who has made us sufficient to be ministers of a new covenant.

Now it gets tricky here, this new covenant business, because Paul sometimes so loves what God has done in Christ that he is ready to brush aside what God does along with Christ.

Where, in Matthew, Jesus tells his disciples to make disciples and to teach the law as Jesus has interpreted the law, Paul sometimes sounds as if he thinks the best way to get to God is to leave the law behind. For Matthew, Jesus is the great interpreter of the law, and for Paul Jesus is the great alternative.

Yet even when Paul looks like he's moving beyond the Hebrew Bible of his youth, he uses the Hebrew Bible to explain that move. When he wants to talk about the new covenant, he turns quickly to the old covenant, to Jeremiah talking about the law written on our hearts. On those days when he's not utterly polemical, Paul knows perfectly well that the God who shines in our hearts through Jesus Christ is the same God who said, "Let light shine out of darkness," and who also said, "Hear O Israel, the Lord your God, the Lord is one."

For some of us here it is God incarnate in Jesus Christ who alone is sufficient, for some of us the God of Abraham, God whom Jesus called "Father" provides the adequacy for which we long. There is a word in Paul for all of us: "Not that we are competent of ourselves to claim anything as coming from us; our competence is from God."

Paul hates to boast except when he's driven to it, and when he's driven to it, he hedges his homiletical bets, tries hard not to become the hero of his own story. Later in this same letter Paul brings testimony to the grace of God, and knows it's also testimony about himself. "If I must boast I will boast of my weakness."

I try to learn from the master. Testimony as confession.

Many years ago I crashed against the wall of my own incompetence. I had come out of high school thinking I was king of the hill, only to arrive at a college populated almost entirely by people equally convinced of their own royalty, equally self-confident and often with better reason.

What had come easy now came hard; good grades, good friends.

Driven at last by grace to something like despair I opened the little book the youth minister of our church had given me as a parting gift, and I found there the words that I do not think are really there but were the words that got me through that night, and many nights and days beyond: "You are not asked to be sufficient."

You are not asked to be sufficient.

I do not need to boast, says Paul, but if I do boast, I shall boast in my weakness and in the power of the Lord.

III

I don't need to boast says Paul, slightly boastfully, Christ is our credential, God is our sufficiency, and then, almost as mysterious, almost as marvelous: "You yourselves are our letter, written on our hearts; to be known and read by all."

We all know about Paul the apostle sent from God. Risen Christ, road to Damascus, bright light, clear voice.

We sometimes forget Paul the pastor, sent to Corinth and Thessalonica and all the rest. Credentialed, apostled, not only by his call, credentialed by his compassion, too.

Thirty-six years ago Robert Clyde Johnson, Dean of Yale Divinity School, stood on this Quad and quoted Paul entirely out of context but to excellent effect. Speaking to the graduates he quoted Romans: "Now the gifts and the call are irrevocable." Paul means the gifts and call to the Jewish people were irrevocable—it was one of Paul's better days. Dean Johnson meant the gifts and the call of those of us who sat before him, eagerly waiting for our diplomas. I affirm what was affirmed: that call, those gifts, that credential is irrevocable.

But another credential awaits you, too. The people to whom you will minister. Those to whom some of you will preach the Gospel, week after week. Those for whom some of you will consecrate bread and wine. Those whom some of you will visit in their times of deepest joy or saddest grief. Those whom every one of you will teach, some in the classroom, some in the parish, some in all the crowded ways of life where inevitably, inescapably, God's people wait for God's word.

The oppressed who await your deeds of liberation.

The lonely who will depend on you for companionship.

The confused who ask you to walk with them on an inevitably crooked way. They are your credentials, your letters of recommendation.

And you, you beloved, are our credentials. Faculty, staff, administration—you students are our credentials. Not these restored grounds or a balanced budget or a 49% acceptance rate for next year's class.

Not so much the books we do and do not write, the lectures we are or are not invited to give, the *summas, magnas,* or *cum laudes* of whatever description we ever so modestly slip into those biographical sketches we hand to the poor pastor or professor who is supposed to introduce us to the audience.

You are our credentials. If I should boast, I boast for all of us who know you.

A few instances stand for the whole. Sitting with Professors Kelsey and Spinks in the Introduction to Ministry class, when we invite parish ministers a few years graduated from this place to talk about their ministry: watching the pastors' honesty, and their humor and their faithfulness. They are proof of God's sufficiency, but they also rightly make us proud. Credentials.

I have been here long enough that people who were students in my early years of teaching have now become colleagues: Carolyn Sharp, Christopher Beeley, Jeremy Hultin, Vicki Hoffer, and others at colleges and seminaries and universities around the world. Credentials.

On Sunday mornings when the Bartletts have the good sense to get to church, I listen to a former student become my pastor preach the Gospel which is really Gospel. Credentials.

An astonishing e-mail list serve from the YDS class of '93 arrives every so often to tell me of pastors and teachers—but also of lawyers and politicians, physicians, public school teachers, church musicians, social workers, spouses, lovers, parents whose being and whose relating have been shaped by this place and by these people. Credentials.

Christ is our credential, says Paul to the Corinthians, but p.s., dear Corinthians, so are you.

Let those who boast boast in the Lord, says Paul, and then of course he boasts on his parishioners, his students, his friends.

On this day as on so many others we learn from the great apostle.

We boast in the Lord.

And, by God, we boast in you.

To Christ be thanks and praise.

Amen.